LEFT AT THE POST

Books by Nicholas von Hoffman:

Mississippi Notebook
The Multiversity
We Are the People Our Parents
    Warned Us Against
Two, Three, Many More (a novel)
Left at the Post

Nicholas von Hoffman

LEFT AT THE POST

Foreword by Benjamin C. Bradlee

Chicago
QUADRANGLE BOOKS
1970

Library of Congress Catalog Card Number: 70-116091

SBN 8129–0142–8

Designed by Joan Stoliar

To
Alexander,
Aristodemos,
and
Constantine

I would like to thank Susan Dooley for editorial help and Mrs. Margaret Weiskopf who prepared this manuscript. These writings appeared originally in the *Washington Post* in 1969 and 1970.

Foreword

In this age of anguish, editors easily become paranoid. The same day's mail can produce angry charges of knee-jerk liberalism and going into the tank for the Establishment, of anti-Semitism and anti-Catholicism, of selling America short and selling out its discontented.

In my own paranoia, I am often tempted to view Nicholas von Hoffman with what could be politely called suspicion. Late in the afternoon, after a day spent disruptively engaging the staff in small talk, he finally sits down to his typewriter. What four-letter word will he try to slip by an editor too innocent to question, or too eager to be an accomplice? What ox has he singled out for his special goring today? What public enemy will he rescue with his special praise? What public hero will he savage with his special sarcasm? And why the hell is he never around to answer the telephone calls and the letters that his columns invariably produce?

But the temptation to suspicion of von Hoffman is to be resisted. For wherever an honest, idealistic man is vaguely uncomfortable with society, there is Nicholas von Hoffman forcing him to focus on his discomfort. Whenever a man drifts wishfully into thinking that he understands things, there is von Hoffman reminding him

"how hideously varied is this pluralistic society." He is at home on the outer perimeters of
our times, where the best of us are exploring new
frontiers in confusion. He gives us the bad dream
of the good America, hiding common sense behind outrage.

If the truth be known, Nick von Hoffman can't
write a news story to save his prematurely gray
head. A case in point involves his assignment to
cover the march of James Meredith across Mississippi in 1966 for the *Washington Post*. His files
would inevitably start with a paragraph or two
reeking of local sociology—two rednecks reliev-
ing themselves against the cinder-block wall of
some filling station at the baked crossroads of
nowhere. The scene-setter would inevitably be
followed by some vintage vernacular, challeng-
ing an editor's standards of taste. (Von Hoffman
has the best ear in the business for American vernacular.) But if Meredith's name appeared in the
copy, it was purely an accident; there would be
no normal time frame, and Nick always did feel
that exact geography was barely relevant. An
editor always had to write a lead to the story,
explaining to the readers that this was a piece
about James Meredith, that he was walking
across the breadth of Mississippi, and that the
events occurred yesterday. Only then were the
rednecks allowed to relieve themselves.

But von Hoffman's dispatches as written were
landmarks in the early, timid years of the new
journalism: personal, pertinent, articulate, vital
glimpses of man trying to make it in a more and
more complicated world. Loosely defined and
loosely practiced, the new journalism has been
much criticized. It interests itself in trees, not
forests, and when you can't see the forest for the
trees, according to the experts, you are in trouble.
But is that true today? I think not, or at least not
necessarily and not generally. Our goal in
journalism is still truth, absolute truth. But truth

today is harder and harder to define, harder and harder to know. Today's truth is all too often tomorrow's half-truth, or even tomorrow's falsity. The most qualified expert can give the most able reporter in town his version of the truth on one day, and yet even that expert can lack one piece of information that makes this truth false the next day. The war in Vietnam has produced enough examples of this equation to boggle the mind.

An in-depth, insightful, subjective, close-in look at one tree—advertised as no more, no less than that—often more closely mirrors the truth than a scholarly look at the forest. And this is what the new journalism is about, even when the new journalist changes from reporter to columnist and opinion is permitted to rear its iconoclastic head.

For Nicholas von Hoffman is the truest American iconoclast since H. L. Mencken. He tilts at more cherished beliefs and more traditional institutions more effectively than anyone since the bad boy of Baltimore. The columns that follow first appeared in the *Washington Post.* They are not for everyone—not for those who feel that all's right with the world, not for those whose cows are sacred, and surely not for those who fear the violent contradictions of our time. Rather they are for those who agree with Justice Oliver Wendell Holmes, Jr., that it is "required of a man that he should share the passion and action of his time at peril of being judged not to have lived."

Benjamin C. Bradlee

LEFT AT THE POST

For over a year I've been writing a column which has elicited a small bit of controversy. Some days the *Washington Post* and I will get thirty or forty letters and as many phone calls. Really not much when you consider the size of the circulation, but a lot for any newspaper, an institution that has come to consider an inert, unresponsive readership a desideratum.

Regardless of which side the phone callers and letterwriters have been on—for or against my firing—they all suggest that it is unusual to find a column like this in a major metropolitan daily. For some its existence is a source of continuing outrage, while others disbelieve that ardent and personal expression could find so conspicuous a place.

Both points of view carry an implicit and unflattering definition of American newspapers. The antis seem to be saying that they've been brought up with a paper which isn't going to tell them anything they don't want to hear. The pros are implying that anything agreeable they read in the papers is unlooked for and unexpected.

For both positions, the underlying meaning is that any newspaper is a highly predictable commodity, the general shape and content of which is known in advance.

What most people call "objective" newswriting is actually being able to predict form and content. We're at home with it so it appears neutral and unbiased, like the living room sofa or the paint on the dining room walls.

We're so at ease with the traditional American newspaper that millions of people who've never been in a newsroom or taken a journalism course know the rules for writing the standard objective American news story: the first sentence should include the four W's—who, what, where, and when—and the rest of the story should be written with all the facts in descending order of importance so if it's too long somebody in the composing room can chop it from the bottom without doing fatal damage to meaning.

Study will reveal that this kind of writing is as biased as any other. An unstated bias decides, for instance, that the important "who" in the first sentence of the moon story should be the three astronauts and not the engineers who did most of the work but who show up many paragraphs down below or in relatively minor side stories. Some of this bias is accidental and historical.

The great terrestrial voyages of discovery depended on their captains and crews. The naval architects of five hundred years ago absolutely had to have the Columbuses and Magellans to sail their ships. The engineers who put men on the moon could have used machines to perform the same tasks, although a robot planting the American flag or hip-hopping around picking up stones or standing at attention when the call came through from the White House would have made a duller TV program.

The bias in our moon coverage arose partly out of passing political need for heroes because of Vietnam, but more deeply out of our American secular religion which ascribes success to the single man's fortitude, the isolated individual's entrepreneurial daring. So, although the astronauts themselves were at pains to explain what a vast collective, corporate effort the flight was, the mass media depicted them as lonely heroes, the Lindberghs or Marco Polos of space.

The modern, anonymous, technological organization, the real "who" of the moon voyage, is too depersonalized to be chivvied into the standard lead sentence. Form and content would have had to be changed to accommodate this different but equally biased way of describing the event.

Many of the television programs and newspaper stories did talk about teamwork, know-how, and organization, but here the tendency was to mix these ideas up into speechifying and preening about what a splendid American accomplishment it was.

Indeed, one of the least remarked upon but most pronounced currents of bias in our news coverage was our glorification of ourselves. Visiting foreigners, unlucky enough to be doused by our accounts of our magnificent exploits, would have to be forgiven a little irritated retching. So many sentences hooking up the American name with high-sounding and sweeping expressions like "all mankind," "not since the invention of the wheel," or "new epoch for humanity."

All of this is very reassuring, and one of the things that the mass media does is reassure, tell people everything is okay, that we're a happy, united, prosperous, generous people, an unmitigated boon to ourselves and the rest of the people on the globe. We need some of this. If we only tell each other we're devils, we may only act like devils, but increasingly this job of national soothing and ego-building has become television's. Once newspapers did it, but never as quickly or completely because there were always a few newspapers who'd "tell the truth and raise hell," to quote some forgotten but probably unpopular editor. There are no maverick television stations. Oh, here and there you'll find one with a little different slant, but for practical purposes they're all the same—bland, cautious, unifying, and conservative without being too nasty about it.

Once movies, too, played this reassuring, unifying role. They glorified the government and the economic system; they recruited for the armed forces and thought they were being terribly brave if they suggested we suffered from uglinesses like anti-semitism. Now it's TV that has to carry that load, to tell you to buy war bonds, join the marines, or fight for better schools by sending to Washington for a pamphlet. The movies and papers have had this heavy, mediocritizing burden taken off them.

Movies, because they're competitively more vulnerable, responded more quickly to liberation. The newspapers—perhaps because a big TV news story sells papers—have gone on fulfilling a function that's been technologically usurped, which TV may do so well it's dangerous. Papers, for the most part, are worse than ever because they're the same.

You can't find a newsreel in a movie theater any more. The movies have given up doing the four W's, but they're more contemporary than they were.

They can come out with a flick like "Medium Cool" a year after the Chicago Convention and be up to date. The reason they can is that the best moviemakers know that if nobody can compete with TV on the four W's, the four W's do not describe reality for modern, particularly college-educated, Americans.

They don't see an event as a discrete act. Rightly or wrongly, they're so permeated with psychological and sociological understanding that for them an event is a complicated environmental sphere of thought, experience, mood, and motif. The TV news leaves them as dissatisfied as the TV drama, so they go to the movies and the movies they see lack conventional plots (the W's of fiction) and run on in seas of total feeling and understanding. What's the plot of "Blow-Up" or "Midnight Cowboy" or "Easy Rider"?

The closest newspapers come to reacting to the new definition of the content of a news event are those incredibly dull trend stories which the writers hate, which the editors publish as a public service, and which the public is smart enough to ignore.

On top of that, history is playing tricks on us. Important news events are beginning to lose their four-W characteristics. The most recent example is Woodstock, where a third of a million people turned out for a concert which nobody could hear and no music reviewers did a criticism of. The *New York Times* handled the story in a four-W way, as it would a Jets-Giants game, with the result that it misled everyone, including its own editorial page. The editorial page has reversed itself, and the paper has printed God knows how many thousands of extra column inches trying to catch up with its own manhandling of the material. It has yet to do it because it's still trapped way back down there in the W's.

Papers don't have to be so out of phase. Over the years, for instance, the *Washington Post* has been evolving into something else. Precisely what is unclear, because it's easier to recognize what a bad newspaper is than to define what a good one ought to be.

We move with hesitation not only because we can make pots of money doing things the old way, but also because we're not sure about our readers. Will they accept a unisexual paper where women are not segregated into a bubble-headed section where every effort is made to present fashion, food, medicine, styles, children vapid and voided of meaning? Do they simply want recipes or do they want to know that some of the food they buy is poisoned?

Can we bring ourselves to lead the paper on a major story with a sidebar? Can we find the people who can see a baseball story the way *Sports Illustrated* does? Can we bring ourselves to understand that a single view of an event—a war or a dip in the stock market— is too simplistic to be acceptable outside of TV?

Television and the newspapers of the past present news in segmented, separated ways which sabotage all but the most conventional received understandings inherited from our parents. By keeping the news split up and disorganized, we force people to choose between explaining their life situation by traditional social mythology or existing in confusion.

When we turn on the tube, we know what we'll get; if the same continues to be true of newspapers, if they can't find it in themselves to surprise and enrich our understanding, we shall be happy now and surprised later in the instant before extinction.   ■

When you've seen one, you've seen 'em all, these welfare ladies, fat from too much starch and too little protein, always out of breath, climbing the stairs by getting one foot up on the next step and then pushing down on the knee. That's how they get up to the second floor of the National Welfare Rights Office, just a few of them, back in town to fulfill the scriptural injunction to be with us always, even unto and beyond National Togetherness Week.

Since the assassination of Aunt Jemima in the late 1950's, fat black women have had only one moment of national acceptance. That came with Fanny Lou Hamer on television before the Democrats in 1964 saying, "I'm so tired of being tired," but quickly the country got tired of her being tired of being tired. The black women never have anything new and interesting to say. Always it's the same, they're poor, no rent money, nothing for the children. It's finally infuriating, like the uncooperative stubbornness of a bed-ridden relative who refuses to die and save the family aggravation and medical bills.

One of the first to arrive at the Headquarters of what has to be the weakest lobby in Washington was Mrs. Geraldine Smith, the financial secretary. She sat down and assumed the slumped, slightly sad, slightly abstracted expression these women get when they wait in clinics, in supermarkets, at bus stops, and in laundromats. Half their lives are given over to waiting. She didn't look at the signs on the walls. "HUELGA—DON'T BUY GRAPES—MOTHER POWER—SAVE LIVES, NOT FACES—JOIN WITH MRS. MARTIN LUTHER KING, SUNDAY, MAY 12, 1968."

She's from Jackson, Mississippi, and she and the other officers of NWRO are here to get an appointment with the new secretary of HEW. There was a little confusion in the room as to who that might be, nothing to be remarked at since even Mr. Nixon has had difficulty remembering the names of those vivid, extra-dimensional men of long mouth and anonymous face who compose his Cabinet.

Mrs. Etta Horn, NWRO's first vice-president, a Washington resident, came into the room and there was a discussion of the black nonpresence at the Inauguration. Downstairs, George Wiley, the group's executive director, was calling around to Robert Finch's office and the White House to see if he or Patrick Moynihan, the President's urbanologist in residence, would be available.

"Wasn't one of those ministers who prayed over him a black man?" somebody asked.

"Only black man I saw in that Inauguration," answered Mrs. Horn, "was the man who opened the door to let him in the White House."

"I'm getting worried about those astronauts," Mrs. Smith remarked. "You know, the Russians don't like black folks any better than we do. I think they're fixin' to put black folks up on the moon."

"How are they going to strap them in?" Mrs. Horn wanted to know.

Saturday night the out-of-town ladies were invited over to a local member's house for supper. Mrs. Qunnie McClain says things are pretty good for her because the coal furnace in her kitchen is so good they sometimes even have to open the windows in the cold weather. "This used to be a wonderful neighborhood," Mrs. McClain said of the deadening, dilapidated area, "but now we're scared to walk the streets."

While the ladies from the local Washington chapter prepared the traditional food—greens, chicken, corn, etc.—for their guests, Mrs. Johnnie Tillmon, the organization's national president, talked to another Mrs. Smith. This Mrs. Smith is the wife of Rev. Griffin S. Smith of the Foundation Baptist Church. "If you're home eleven o'clock Sunday morning listen to our radio program. It's on WUST. We have it for the sick and shut-in and we have quite a few lovely donors. We're tax-free and thank God for that," the minister's wife said.

She and Mrs. Tillmon discussed the length of skirts and sexual morals in general. You had the impression that Mrs. Smith was rather inclined toward a Nixonian view. "I know a Muslim boy," she said, "I don't share his religion. I pray for him, but I agree with him because he says a woman should be covered and a man should have only one wife."

Mrs. Tillmon took that in and replied, "They say during the war skirts go up. I wasn't here for World War I. I know they went up in World War II, but this war, well, baby—!"

Before eating, Mr. Smith said the blessing and his wife asked everyone to sing one chorus of "The Lord Is Blessing Me Right Now," which everybody did, and even the people who didn't know the words hummed along. There wasn't nearly enough room at the table for the whole company, so the ladies took their plates into the living room and George Wiley and the ministers stayed at the table. After dinner, Mrs. Tillmon got a tiny half-pint of Old Fitz out of a bag and poured a little into some of the ladies' cans of Pepsi-Cola. She saw the newspaperman watching her and evidently thought he disapproved.

"We all like what other folks like," she said to him. "We weren't always on welfare. Once we had jobs and homes like other people. Welfare is just our way of surviving. What I'm trying to do now is to see that my daughter's husband doesn't leave her. For that he's gotta have a decent education and earn a decent wage. I'd like to see Tricia Nixon raise a family on $300 a month."

George Wiley told everybody that Moynihan had agreed to see them at the White House today. So this afternoon they'll pull themselves up those stairs, out of breath, to say again what they've been saying for years. ■

A pietistical voice with mellow reverberations in the lower registers asked the people to drop their heads and close their eyes. That is how white occidentals indicate they are addressing their divinity. The TV cameras panned around the new Madison Square Garden, and the multitude—assembled to hear Billy Graham—looked like the Republican party at prayer.

For ten consecutive days Billy, as he refers to himself, was on view over Channel 5 while he presided over his $1 million New York Crusade. The face of the famous evangelist ages without wrinkling; instead of the skin showing the marks of time, the flesh beneath it has began to puff and bulge. Some men get old that way, by gradually turning into superannuated babies, but the process isn't that far advanced with Billy. He is still recognizably God's pretty, curly-haired boy.

When people who don't like Billy write about him, they tend to imply he's a modern, slicked-over Elmer Gantry. They like to talk about the money he takes in, but they have him all wrong. He isn't a jack-leg preacher with a good tailor and a clever CPA. It's a straight operation, and as much as people have looked they haven't found a trace of evidence that he lives any better than or even as well as many a bishop or minister to a rich, fashionable congregation.

Billy, more than Norman Vincent Peale, is America's court preacher. Our Bossuet, the cleric invited to the palaces to preach to the king. In him we can see the formal union of state, society, and religion, the working partnership between God and Caesar, not rendering to each other so much as washing each other's hands.

Usually when the formal, ruling part of society is thus able to harness God for its own day-to-day purposes, when it's able to coopt the symbols of life and eternity, the result has been to empty out the churches and make disbelievers. The centuries of collusion between the thrones of England, France, and Russia and their respective churches ultimately destroyed the masses' faith. The reports from around this country show a continuous heavy drop-off in church attendance. Even the clergymen are quitting in unprecedented numbers.

Billy is in high regard at the White House and in other centers of power. Businessmen work with him to ensure he can appear an hour a night on television. They should, for he preaches a doctrine of unmitigated submission to all arrangements, social, economic, and political. He tells you by going to Bible school, by being obedient, by handing out tracts, by doing nothing that is threatening or that could possibly change anything, Jesus will love you in life and console you in death.

Billy is a reactionary, but not a stupid one. He recognizes the enormous concern there is for poverty and racism and war. In his preaching he picks up on it and then misleads his listeners into accepting it:

"You know that's a problem we face in our world today, the problem of poverty. It causes an ache in my heart all the time . . . the pet dogs, our animal friends in America live a far higher standard of living than millions of people in other parts of the world. You know the Bible teaches we have a responsibility to the poor. Proverbs 21/13: 'Whoso stoppeth his ears at the cry of the poor, he also shall cry himself, but shall not be heard.' "

But does this statement lead to action? Not at all, because it is shortly followed by the meat of his message:

"Now according to the standard they've laid out, I was reared in poverty. I didn't know it. No-

body came along and told me. I didn't watch a
television program and see what a great problem
I'd become. [So much for you, CBS, with your
exposés of hunger.] All I knew to do was to go
out and work from three o'clock in the morning
till sundown . . . I've found a lot of people who
don't really want to work, and the Bible says in
Second Thessalonians 3/10, 'If any will not
work, neither shall he eat.' I saw a sign the other
day. It said, 'I FIGHT POVERTY, I WORK.' "

If you haven't gotten the idea that the best way
to fight poverty is to enrich yourself, Billy will
tell you that an unseemly regard for the poor is
reason to suspect that you're a scoundrel:

"You know Judas had a great burden for the
poor. When Mary Magdalen anointed the feet of
Jesus with an expensive ointment, Judas was
angry and said, 'Lord, why didn't we take this
money and give it to the poor?' . . . Judas wasn't
concerned about the poor, because he was a
thief. He wanted it for himself. Many people
carry a heavy load for poverty because they want
votes, and others want to get involved in the
problems so they can get their hand in the till,
but that should never do away with our responsibility for the legitimate poor."

What that responsibility is Billy never says
even when he has a perfect opportunity to give
some concrete advice: ". . . There's a dignity to
working with your hands. There's a dignity to
cleaning the street. There's dignity to carrying
the garbage. Don't be ashamed of that. If you're
a Christian you can throw your shoulders back
and say, 'Yes, sir, I'm a garbage collector and I'm
proud of it.' "

But Billy Graham wasn't in Memphis when
Martin Luther King marched and died to help
those garbage collectors gain the Christian dignity that Billy Graham says is rightfully theirs.
Moreover, nobody who would take Billy Graham

at his word would ever lift a hand to help anybody.

Be submissive, know your place, avoid collective action, accept, accept everything as it is and most of all Jesus: "There's dignity to being a maid . . . in God's sight it has dignity to it . . . You talk about soul brothers! When you come to Christ you have got some soul brothers and black is beautiful and white is beautiful and yellow is beautiful and red is beautiful!"

And while he was speaking these cruel words, Ralph Abernathy, the fool of God, who does resemble many of the Old Testament figures Billy loves to talk about, was stumbling through the streets of Charleston, South Carolina, being arrested, attempting to win dignity for maids and garbage collectors, not in God's sight, but their own. ■■■

When faith comes to be separated from life by its believers, when they begin to look at it as one religion in a world containing many, it's on its way out. For when faith becomes religion, something overlapping but apart from reality as the believer perceives it, it has turned into a creed or a tradition or a set of ethical precepts or a puzzling metaphysical bestiary to be argued over, reconciled with, asserted, defended, lived by, or passed on to one's children as a cultural heirloom.

Christianity is passing through this progression from faith to religion to a probable extinction. Christians no longer cohabit a universe rich with a marvelous variety of metaphysical beings. The devils and demons that were once as real to Christians as the Dow-Jones averages are to us are gone. If His Satanic Majesty endures at all, it is probably as the name of a rock and roll band. The good angels are the property of Hallmark greeting cards.

If Billy Graham and the Pope still refer to an anthropomorphic male divinity who has a beard longer than a hippy's and sits on a sky throne, the theologians from the classier divinity schools squirm, apologize, and ask us to look at the Bible as allegory. Even Paul VI has found it expedient to commit euthanasia on a whole clotch of saints, declaring that they never did have life and expunging them from the canons. Yet once they were at least as alive and vivid as the present occupant of the White House, probably more so.

Christianity, however, doesn't extinguish itself at the same rate of speed and in the same way in the hearts of all people. For some, rural people in other countries, it remains what it was during the period churchmen call "the age of faith." In America, the religious ardor of social strata and cultural subgroups cools at varying rates, thus contributing to the argufying friction in our national life.

Women appear to hold onto religion longer than men. Republicans seem to give it up more slowly than liberal Democrats. Members of the American Medical Association, tool and die makers, United States Congressmen, taxicab drivers, and assistant office managers appear to remain believers longer than English professors, social workers, clergymen, college students, the very poor, and the socially concerned among the very rich.

Even though Christianity is now shut up in its churches, relegated to being a specialized activity, no longer invisible as when faith and daily life were one and indistinguishable, even if it's shamefully used to sanctify the most diabolic practices, millions of people stick with it. Some because they believe, some for the same reason they fly back from the Bahamas at the end of December—they can't imagine Christmas without snow and pine trees. Some move away gradually, going from the orthodox churches to halfway houses like the Presbyterians before they or their children drop off entirely via Unitarianism or ethical culture.

Where do these fadeaways go? There's been a lot of publicity about Zen and trips to India or astrology, but many of them simply go to psychology. Psychology can be such a total faith that you don't know you're a believer; you absorb the psychological way of looking at things so completely that most of the time you're unaware of what you're doing.

"Everything is seen, 'understood,' and acted upon in terms of depth drama actually or possibly underlying any act; little behavior is taken at face value; almost without consciousness of alternative possibilities of perception, everything very nearly is 'interpreted,'" writes John R. Seeley in *The Americanization of the Unconscious* (International Science Press, 1967). It is a good description of how the faith operates in psychological man. The important thing about him is the processes of his faith, not its specific doctrinal content.

In rare instances he may have a specific creed. He may be a Freudian or a Rogerian or a you-name-it, but what distinguishes him from others is how he looks at himself and the world. Psychological man seeks not grace but an illusive, furtive self whom he can never catch up with, though he chases him forever down the silvered tubes of his own mind where every shape is a reflection. To find himself he will go to psychodramas, take sensitivity training, plunge into nude encounter groups, subject himself to forty-eight-hour, nonstop marathons, pay thousands of dollars for analysis, subject himself to attack therapy. He loves to be theraped the way monks once loved to be scourged, not because he's sick but because he's seeking.

What he honors and looks for he can experience but he can never possess, because they're qualities and states of mind that come and go. He's forsworn earlier ideas like adjustment and maturity because his teacher, his boss, his parents, even his sergeant have found out they can use them to keep him in line and miserable. Instead he quests for "development," for "openness" and "awareness." He's like a chick in an opaque, gelatinous, plastic egg, pecking to get out, but his beak can't find anything hard to strike against and crack open.

He believes he has a self as matter of factly as Burgundian peasants once believed they had immortal souls. The self and soul are different. The soul was immortal, highly structured, and unchanging. The self is in a personality warp, to borrow an expression from science fiction. It can assume many faces, play many roles, even at the same time. Psychological man sees himself not as a father, office worker, softball player, husband, but as one who plays the role of father, office worker, etc. Yet the more roles the self plays, the more it can do on the personality warp, the more difficult it is to grab hold of and understand.

Psychological man doesn't leave off operating this way with himself, but uses his thinking in relation to others and public affairs. You can get a whiff of it in the Southern complaint that the Warren Supreme Court gave up law for sociology, which is but another way of saying they gave up naming and categorizing things for "understanding" them in the manner that psychological man characteristically does.

The same conflict has come into play in regard

to crime. Biblical man asserts standards; psychological man asserts norms that move around like a grading curve or line on an oscilloscope. Biblical man wants to punish; psychological man wants to understand and perchance therap.

Sometimes, however, psychological man's way of looking at things is convenient to the dishonest members of Biblical man's dying order. Psychological man with his intense interest in understanding often fails to recognize man's ancient cupidities. Hence, you seldom hear people speculate that a public official has been bribed anymore. Psychological man doesn't think that way, and some of the Biblical men around town are just as happy.

Not all the people who've left the Christian churches are becoming adherents of the religion of psychology, although few of us—except White House aides and members of the Liberty League—are completely untouched. It's too pervasive, too triumphant, too insidious, too much in the air to ward off. The result is an invisible division that is seldom discussed but which complicates and embitters every attempt to find a new set of social ground rules we can agree on. ■

The Pope has told his cardinals to take off the red shoes with the silver buckles. Henceforth they're to be addressed as "My Lord Cardinal" instead of "Your Eminence." They still get to have coats of arms as long as they conform to the rules of heraldry.

If you're a low church democrat, you may consider these changes something short of earth-shaking. They're nevertheless noteworthy as an example of institutional accommodation to a growing irreverence and disrespect for authority. The Catholic Church has got so much of it the Pope recently said it is suffering "from an agitation that is practically schismatic" deriving from "groups that are jealous of an arbitrary, and at root selfish, autonomy, masked as Christian pluralism or freedom of conscience."

The Pope voices his complaint in his Latinate way, but presidents, generals, university chancellors, labor bosses, businessmen, and parents are saying the same thing in less orotund language. It does little good. Once authority loses the magic circle of unquestioning respect it's impossible to lecture people back into their former state of mind.

You can try to shame people for their lack of respect, tell them they're immature or that they're ungrateful, but once the thread is broken force is usually needed to exact obedience. A good example of this was provided on a call-in radio talk show where the host, Howard Nelson, had Father Henry Ouellette on his program. Cardinal Richard Cushing of Boston happened to tune in and was bothered enough by what was said to call up and order the priest off the air.

Cardinal Cushing: "Father Ouellette, who paid for your education? . . . The Archdiocese of Boston."

Father Ouellette: "That's right, Your Eminence."

Cardinal Cushing: "You are upsetting the people of the Catholic Church, my dear Father. We've paid for your education. I pay for this stuff."

Father Ouellette: "Your Eminence, I was asked to come here as a psychologist."

Cardinal Cushing: "For goodness sakes, get off that program."

Nelson: "One of our functions, Cardinal Cushing, is to bring all kinds of information to a radio audience."

Cardinal Cushing: "Wait a minute. He's confusing all the Catholic people. I've been very good to that station, WEEI."

Nelson: "I think we have contributed a great deal to the greater Boston area with the help of a very fine, top-notch psychologist, Father Ouellette."

Cardinal Cushing: "Suppose I pull him off of there?"

Father Ouellette: "Your Eminence, I've tried to be an educator."

Cardinal Cushing: "You're wrecking—you're, you're, you're downgrading the Catholic Church. . . . The country's in bad shape. Why don't you talk about politics? Why don't you talk about taxes?"

The Cardinal succeeded in getting his priest off the air, but usually when respect for authority is gone, little short of physical coercion will work. It is believed three thousand or more American priests quit the Catholic Church in 1968 alone.

We may not have yet moved to the point where we have a full-blown crisis of authority. There are still plenty of people who believe President Nixon has a secret peace plan on no more evidence than when the President says something it's true. They revere the office to the point of disbelieving any occupant could tell a lie.

At the same time there are a growing number of people who will accept the words of neither Pope nor President if they're spoken ex cathedra and are meant to be taken on faith without proof. These are the ones that are causing the trouble by asking of all who issue orders, "Well, why should he boss me?"

The bosses of this world have begun to look around for new ways to legitimize their authority. However, the mood at the moment makes it difficult to legitimize authority without sharing it. The Pope can tell the cardinals to take off their red shoes, but is such a gesture enough to keep another three thousand priests from taking off their collars?

The government can promise "participation" in the ghettos, the President can assure the "little man" his wishes are being intuited, college presidents can form consultative bodies with their students, but all of this is just a way of telling the secular cardinals in the nonchurch bureaucracies to throw away their red shoes and stash their princely airs and arrogances. It won't work for long. It wasn't the shoes that brought authority into disrespect. It was only after people had started talking back to the boss without feeling guilty that they noticed he looked a little silly in those funny, old-fashioned shoes.   ▬

It used to be that the only way a kid could find out what the top half of a grown-up girl looked like was to read the *National Geographic.*

Even there, the nether regions of the human body were hidden by loincloths, bushes, and palm leaves. A normally curious child has greater access to photographs of the surface of the planet Mars than of the surfaces of other members of his species.

As a result, millions of Americans associate sex with the tropics, primitive people, and anthropology, a fact that may explain the reluctance of some members of Congress to help underdeveloped countries to industrialize.

The total banishment of the nude from polite

society is the foundation upon which the girlie magazine and nudie movie industry has been built.

You can expect that long after even the Baptists and the Roman Catholics have given up the fight, the leaders of these industries will be carrying on the battle for censorship.

Today pictures of the top half of people are readily accessible.

There are lots of still photographs in magazines like Vogue, and, if you want live, breathing color, go to a movie, any movie.

Even the newspapers are loosening up a little. Many no longer airbrush out belly buttons, so that we have ceased to look like a race of Adams, although representations of other parts of the female are still considered unprintable.

We continue to take a very strong position on what's happening below the waistline. In this sphere, there is no discussion of a flexible response, so that in all likelihood we will recognize Red China before we recognize certain areas of the human anatomy.

When the Beatles remarked they thought they were somewhat more popular than Jesus Christ, the flap was mild compared with what happened when John Lennon and his girl friend, Yoko Ono, had themselves photographed in the nude on a record-album cover. (This may not be a fair test inasmuch as the two of them are so ugly the rumor is going around they are actually undercover agents for Hart, Shaffner & Marx.)

Words, even Latin words, for parts of the human and animal anatomy have a hard time making it into print without being burned or confiscated. This is changing somewhat.

Publications like *Harper's* and the *Atlantic Monthly* now permit the use of any word in the English language, including America's favorite four-letter obscenity, an expression that is so old the sixth edition of the *Dictionary of Slang* suggests its origin is a Greek verb. The conventions of daily journalism prevent your being given any more hints than these.

The practice of the *Washington Post* prohibits the use of a long and indeterminate list of words standing for parts of the human body, and describing many acts necessary to sustain as well as procreate life itself. At the time of the Chicago convention, the *Post* and other newspapers would not print the epithets being exchanged by demonstrators and policemen.

Many people, especially radical, liberal types, object to these strictures. Why, they argue, should people have to conform to Calvinist morality when they don't believe in the Calvinist or any other God?

They're wrong to take this position. Banning certain words and objects is, in the weird perversity of the logic of human action, a great help in communicating with people.

One of the biggest problems facing the angry people who are thrashing around and coming up with new ideas is that the language but not the substance of their thought is stolen from them. President Nixon goes around making the V sign for peace. Flatulent politicians look you straight in the eye and begin their speeches by saying, "First, let's get down to the nitty gritty." The underarm-deodorant people sell their sprays by telling you they "know where the action is." There is even a Dodge rebellion.

This is disastrous for communication. If the top dog is going to bark like the underdog, how is the weaker of the two ever going to get his demands for justice and change understood?

In our present situation, speech is on the verge of being rendered meaningless. That is why some radicals would just as soon see the First Amendment destroyed along with the Fifth, as former presidential candidate Thomas E. Dewey has proposed.

Thanks to the historical aversion to dirty words of the ruling groups in our society, nothing so drastic is needed. People are able to couch their thoughts in disagreeable, obscene terms, which no advertising agency or U.S. Senator would dare copy and absorb into public rhetoric.

The judicious use of four-letter words restores meaning to what the politicians, aping the radical clergy, call dialogue. Obscenity sets up the possibility of having real discussions about real disagreements, because dirty words make it impossible to disguise disagreement and claim consensus where none exists.

Nudity works the same way. Taking off your clothes in public is an extraordinarily successful method of protest in a time when public officials are inured to demonstrations no matter how large their size. A case in point is the middle-echelon government girl who tells this story:

"I work for a man who's much older than me. We disagree on almost everything, but he refuses to recognize this fact. He wears long sideburns and modified hip clothes. He's always telling me I'm cool and that he's really on my side. The next time he does, instead of fighting with him, I'm not going to say anything. I'm just going to strip and see if he does that, too."

As our leading men never tire of telling us, we have much in our Puritan heritage to be thankful for. ▰▰

"T"hey" have suppressed the people's music again. This time it happened at a Georgetown joint called Emergency, a nonalcoholic place. The official reason was some kind of bureaucratic diddlybop about too much exposed wood. As if the city didn't have the miles of slums with exposed wood, wiring, and cockroaches which the Department of Licenses and Inspections has lived in peace and harmony with for so many years.

They formed a cultural lynch mob to ensure that the people's music—rock, blues, folk, jazz, etc.—wouldn't be played at the Ambassador Theater. This is no Washington phenomenon. It happens all over the country. Even in San Francisco they chased Chet Helms and the Family Dog out of the Avalon Ballroom, thus ending one of our best and most important centers of people's live music.

The people's music, whether it be country and western, early Dixieland, spirituals, or jazz, has always had to fight for a place to play in, respectability, and respect. The fact that millions love it has never helped it escape being consigned to third-rate gin mills on the fringes of society. Some of the best music that's been composed and performed in America in the last ten or fifteen years has come out of a Chicago dive called Pepper's Lounge.

Today you have to drive hundreds of miles to hear good live rock or blues or C&W. There are the pop festivals with their accompanying dangers: cops, hassles, riots, and shucks. Some advertise groups and musicians they haven't signed up. They promise you Cream (disbanded) and serve you Coffeemate.

When an artist is sufficiently old and impotent, when his kind of music has stopped growing and being alive, they'll give him some recognition. Then you'll have one of those insufferable condescending scenes at Carnegie Hall or the White House where an old man will be led out to play some happy birthday riffs for the President. Can't you picture the scene in the White House around 1990: There is Pete Seeger or Bo Diddley in a wheel chair, blind from glaucoma, hands too palsied to pick up a guitar, listening while some President tells them how much they did for their country. Even Eleanor Roosevelt, who appears to have been the only genuinely concerned First Lady in the last forty years, invited Marian Anderson to sing there after black people had long since given up spirituals.

In America the only good music is dead music. Officially, it appears that our greatest composer is Ludwig van Beethoven. Next comes Mozart, Brahms, Bach, etc., etc. This is not to knock them. Theirs is high art and deserves to be played, but not to the point of excluding the music which expresses our times. They wrote for audiences that have been dead for hundreds of years; it makes no more sense to have them jamming up every concert hall than it would to glut all our theaters with Shakespeare and Euripides.

We go even further. We dot our cities with musical museums fit only for performing ancient works. The most recent, which is still abuilding, is that thing called the Kennedy Center which will incorporate a hall for grand opera. You'd best believe it. Presumably this is because there are hundreds of thousands of people in the Washington metropolitan area who can't sleep at night because there is no place for them to go to see *Aida* and the other pop-art classics of nineteenth-century imperialist pomposity.

Kennedy Center is supposed to open in 1970. You know what that occasion will be like. Rich guys in their dinner jackets, their superfluous wives—the same ladies who disport on the women's pages from time to time—government biggies, chauffeurs; champagne, jewels, snobbery, knots of us peasants trying to guess the names of these important people. In deference to the times, there may be a few house Negroes, but in the main it will be a splendid reaffirmation of the least defensible aspects of a creaky and increasingly disfunctional class structure.

The matter is made more irksome because the rich pay scarcely anything for these brilliant, intimidating shows. Much of the money for a joint like Kennedy Center is tax money appropriated by Congress, and the rest is tax deductible. It's tax deductible because it's defined as a worthy cause, something for the general public's good. Aside from the certain probability that the general public will never get near the place, costs of tickets and babysitters being what they are, public good here is actually the private good of a limited number of people comprising a master class.

This is not to say there isn't a public good in having places where Beethoven is performed, but so many? And in so many cities? And while the police power of the state is constantly used to thwart other, far more popular and germane kinds of music? The rest of the world honors and listens to the music that has come out of our cotton fields and our ghettos, but we not only refuse to subsidize it, we act like the bygone Kings of Bavaria paying out money that could support the living to memorialize dead string quartets.

The people who do these things doubtless believe they are supporting the arts and are unaware of how repressive their activities are. Yet, if what is held up as the best art, the highest practices of culture are incomprehensible and arcane, people are pushed down in their own minds; they feel their own art is contemptible and that the good art is encased in mausoleums to be understood only after years of appreciation which demands leisure and opportunities they don't have. In these circumstances art turns into priestcraft, it reinforces hierarchical mind-sets and is perverted into an instrument of social control.

You can get the feel of this in the physical design of these buildings. From the outside they crush you and make you feel small. On the inside we have massive chandeliers, plush, gold curtains, and the proscenium stage with the musicians up there and us down here. It is the lecture hall and pulpit, designed for a certain kind of musical performance, one where they pitch and we catch, where we sit still and listen.

The living music of America can't be played in such places. It must be close to its audience, an audience which is not passive but takes part by clapping, singing, and dancing, where the relationships aren't hierarchical but reciprocal.

To the people who make most of the decisions, such stuff is unnerving. They don't know why, but they sense trouble from the theaters that don't have immutable seating charts. It could spread to a demand for free-form organizational charts, to new intimacies that might squoosh flat our pyramidal social structures. They don't believe it's possible to accomplish our tasks better through relationships of a different quality.

In the meantime, if somebody asks you for a contribution to the Kennedy Center, don't. We have enough stuff like that. Let's let this one rust or plank it over into one large, flat floor suitable for the roller derby, a people's sport. ■■■

Whenever a big demonstration is shaping itself into a fist getting ready to hit, our public wise men come forward with advice for the protesters. Whatever the cause or the occasion, the advice from politicians and editorialists is always the same.

"If you do this, you'll only hurt your own cause. You'll produce a backfire, backlash, backroar, etc." It wouldn't be surprising to learn that the driver of the bus which Rosa Parks integrated in Montgomery, Alabama, so many years ago had attempted to get her back in the segregated section by explaining she was only hurting her own people by carrying on so. All his public life, the Rev. Dr. Martin Luther King was warned that if he sat in, picketed, marched, or tried to register to vote, he ran the risk of setting back the black man.

Who usually gives this advice? The fellows on the other side. The Segs used to say that to Dr. King, and it's the war hawks who say it now to the peaceniks. The source alone makes it suspect. What really is meant by this small bit of statesmanly help is, "If you march and anything bad happens, we'll do our best to blame it on you and get as many people as possible against you for it."

One of the marks of operative political freedom is the liberty to louse up your own cause by poor judgment and bad tactics. We've been over this again and again with the blacks, who've insisted that a white man can't general a black man's cause. If the cause is lost the black man must pay; the same holds true for the peace movement, which essentially is a young people's movement because the burden of the war falls heaviest on them.

Another category of remarks and admonitions centers around "sincerity." There are a number of variants, but the gist is, "If you want to prove your sincerity, you won't march on the grass without a permit, you will submit to arrest and go to jail, or you will act responsibly, i.e., you will do what we want you to do."

If sincerity were a test in politics, nine out of

ten public officeholders would be turned out tomorrow morning. Sincerity is a private virtue,
and people who demand it only demand it of
their enemies. If you disagree with me, the only
way I'll believe you're sincere is if you change
your mind and join me.

Next we have the double-mouthed critic who
wants to get a leg up on both sides. He likes to
say, "Your cause is fine, noble, generous, and
public spirited, but your leaders and/or some of
your followers are terrible. Why don't you throw
out the Communists, radicals, activists, and luna-
tics on your steering committee, and pick some
good, moderate, middle-of-the-road, responsible
people?"

Politics is tough enough without each side let-
ting the other pick its leaders. The blacks have
had to suffer through *this* again and again—
"We're for equality, but we won't negotiate with
militants." Often what this translates into is,
"We don't mind you messing around as long as
the people leading you are compliant and ineffective, but we don't want you being influenced by
some bunch that knows what it's doing."

There is a degree of seeming plausibility to
this criticism. Some of us are jarred and discon-
certed when we learn there are two Communist
party members on the board of a local peace
committee. For people who fear violence, the
presence of CP members should be reassuring.
Old-line Reds tend to be lawnorder types who're
as suspicious of unsupervised, popular demonstrations as any White House aide. But the point
is that there is no way to bar the door to Communists or SDS members or Trotskyites because the
peace movement is a movement, not a political
party.

In American politics the parties are run by
one-half of one per cent of the membership—the
silent minority, you might call it—so they can
control what kind of person is allowed into influ-

ential positions. A social movement, by definition, is a different species of animal. It has no
stability, it shrinks and swells, it takes cues from
people in leadership positions, but its awesome
strength derives from the millions of individuals
making up their own minds to join in. This is why
the government can continue to indict leaders
without any visible effect on the peace movement's strength. It is not controlled by tiny numbers of people who have power to keep out Communists but admit moderates.

Another argument you frequently hear is, "If
you do this there may be violence and the blood
will be on your hands." Sometimes that's true,
but if we look at the history of civil conflict in
the United States it's clear that often the responsibility for blood being shed has to be assumed
by the authorities. Flirtatious delays in issuing
parade permits, the use of *agents provocateurs*
are instances of officials inciting to riot. It hasn't
been the anti-war leaders who have crossed state
lines to give kid-baiting, incendiary talks, and
you know these speakers aren't going to be indicted under the Rap Brown Act.

For a demonstration to remain peaceful, there
must be lawful conduct both from the marchers
and the authorities. If it's true that violence will
hurt the peace movement, then there are others
besides a few demented kids from SDS who
stand to gain by fulminating it.

Next we get to the unity-divisiveness theme.
Somebody gave a classic expression of it on the
tube: "Let us be united for peace. Let us also be
united against defeat. Because let us understand: North Vietnam cannot defeat the United
States. Only Americans can do that."

It is by uttering such words, especially behind
the presidential shield, that a "silent majority" is
created. A silent majority is a large, flaccid glop
of people who thoughtlessly give assent because
the question doesn't matter enough to them to

think it through. People are silent because they are gagged, despairing, or indifferent. This majority is silent because it doesn't care enough.

Taken on their face, these calls for unity make no sense, but they're comprehensible if you understand unity to mean obedience—"Be obedient for peace. Be obedient against defeat." Except in rare moments of self-evident, not government-proclaimed, national crisis, unity is antithetical to the democratic process. Our whole theory of ruling ourselves is based on the assumption that rival ideas and policies must be encouraged to have it out so that we may pick the wisest and best.

We've had thirty years of unity, of bipartisan foreign policies, of obediently cheering, while our presidents roam infinitely about the planet, lamp in hand, like Diogenes, trying to find a peaceful nation. An end to unity. Bring on division and debate. It's terrible on the ears and the nerves, but it's never been claimed that democracy is the easiest form of government, only the best. ▬

When during a war the leader of one side dies, it's customary for the other side to cheer. With the passing of Uncle Ho our cheering has been ragged and hesitating.

Here in the homeland of Uncle Ho's most powerful and dedicated enemies, even here his obituaries have been tinctured with praise and admiration. You get the feeling that the people who hated him because he was a Communist would have traded Uncle Ho for Thieu, Ky, Diem, and several boatloads of the more important cor-ruptionists, dope smugglers, double-agents, de-serters, and liberty-lovers allied with us.

Uncle Ho alone appears to have come out of the war with his reputation. In death he seems the one outstanding man the war has produced. This curiously popular head of an enemy country has even had his communism explained away. "He turned to communism as a means—not an end—to achieve his lifelong goal of freedom and unity for his homeland," said the lead editorial in the *New York Times.*

The pro–Uncle Ho sentiment has been so strong that the other night on NBC Chet Huntley had to remind us not to be carried away. The old man had killed a lot of innocent people, he said, but the same has been said of the American presidents involved in Vietnam.

Our reaction to these massacres is like Kurt Vonnegut's in his novel *Slaughterhouse Five.* "So it goes," he says, because if you meditate on all the death and dying you'll go crazy, the facts'll burn out the eyes of your mind. Uncle Ho killed a lot of people. So it goes. A boy driven mad by the war blows his brains out on the Capitol steps. So it goes.

It was said against Uncle Ho that he was a professional revolutionary. The United States has its professional revolutionaries too. Men like Allen Dulles and Richard Helms, the CIA bosses who differ from Uncle Ho in that he wanted to commit a revolution in his own country while they want to do it in other people's. Uncle Ho was involved in politics so he did what people in that line of work do; what made him different from our bunch were his reasons, or thus it seems, because really we don't know much about him.

We're not even sure what his real name was or if he ever got married. We have some black-and-white newsreel footage, some snapshots, a couple of old police dossiers; we know he was a good cook and a heavy cigarette smoker who made it to seventy-nine. Salems were his brand ... Oh, you can get the Americans out of the war, but you can't get the war out of the Americans. But Ho was probably too busy to think up new words to old advertising jingles.

Maybe if we'd known Uncle Ho better we might not have regarded him with as much respect. The little glimpses make him so attractive. Imagine, a bandy-legged wog, renting a Sunday suit to go out to Versailles to present Wilson and Clemenceau with a petition asking that his distant little colony be granted self-determination ... and years later Uncle Ho still living like a poor man, wearing sandals cut from old automobile tires. There may have been a mean side to him, but we never heard about that. We're left with these brief pictures to match up against our leading men.

Ellsworth Bunker, Ambassador to Vietnam and possessor of a good tailor, back in Washington for consultations as they say, his old eyelids sagging down to make drooping, mysterious triangles of his eyes, murmuring he didn't think he wanted to comment on the repercussions of Uncle Ho's death.

Presidents on airport runways in front of microphones, silvery Air Force One in the background so behind them you can read THE UNITED STATES OF AMERICA, and you can hear the words, presidential words, susceptible of many interpretations by American watchers and White House-ologists from the other side of the iron curtain, peace, commitments, honor, face, freedom, treaties, solemnly pledged, bombing, war.

Or the generals, Westmoreland, handsome nonwinner, all jaw and gold braid, Chapman ordering the black and white Marines to stop killing each other and get back to killing the

Vietnamese (so it goes), and Hershey, doughty seventy-five-year-old conqueror of ten thousand squeamish liberals, givin' it to the kids and telling them what an honor it is.

The kids went for Uncle Ho. "Ho! Ho! Ho Chi Minh!" they'd chant at the big rallies to end the war against him. Recently they haven't been chanting so much. General Hershey's been coming down on them heavy and they've had to spend their energy escaping. All over the country, a million bull sessions about that. Don't get busted for pot in Illinois because they've changed the law so it's only a misdemeanor now and a misdemeanor won't keep you out.

It's gotta be a felony. Steal a car, that's good if it's grand theft auto, but joy riding won't keep you out of anything. Be a teacher or a cop or a fag. Get a sympathetic draft board. Cut off a toe. There's lots of nine-toed guys who don't have any trouble hitting on chicks. You can wear shoes. What chick's going to count your toes? I know but I can't do it. Once I put my foot on the kitchen table and I had the cleaver in my hand, but, man, it was my toe, my toe, man. So get married. Have a dependent. Adopt a baby or a sick old mother.

The kids never blamed Uncle Ho for causing General Hershey to draft so many of them. That was strange, but people never were able to work up a good hate against him. Wall Street didn't blame him for the market's not cracking 1,000 on the Dow-Jones. Remember this was the year it was going to happen? The old people didn't blame him for the inflation. Strange. Strange too, thinking about a truce in a war to mourn the other side's leader. The Americans didn't do that for Hitler. The Germans didn't do that for Roosevelt.

Uncle Ho did that to this war, drained our side of righteousness, left us nothing but the fine print and the technicalities. He had a monopoly on the big phrases, the words you put on banners, so we fought for some sentences written by lawyers and printed in agate type and cheered ourselves on with the thought we have a fine professional army doing the job it was sent out there to do.

Now maybe we'll get a few of the slogans back and a little of the old enthusiasm. Ho had it, but they can't keep it in Hanoi because he's gone, dead, dead like so many others over there are dead. So it goes. ▬

The red men have captured Alcatraz. They're living in the abandoned jail cells, the old dungeons, the forsaken guards' dormitory. The red men have taken the island, the red men whom we thought dead, destroyed as a people, ruined as a culture; they have come out of the earth where for sure we'd buried them, and sailed out from San Francisco a mile and a half across the bay. Now they say they have the island and they won't give it back.

They want it for a pan-Indian cultural center, a place where they can bring the smashed fragments of their heritage, the potsherds of their history, and maybe by pooling what's left of Shoshone, Chippewa, Seminole, Crow, Mohawk, Hopi, and all the other tribes and peoples, they can make a new mosaic of self-knowledge and identity. There are only chips and pieces left to work with, for these red men are the remnants of last century's Pinkvilles.

Yes, there have been other Pinkvilles, other Mylais. No, don't let anybody tell you Pinkville is an "isolated incident." Compare these eyewitness accounts.

First a portion of former Army photographer Ron Haeberle's description of the death of a child as presented in *Life* magazine:

"There was a little boy walking toward us in a daze," says Haeberle. "He'd been shot in the arm and leg. He wasn't crying or making any noise." Haeberle knelt down to photograph the boy. A GI knelt down next to him. "The GI fired three shots into the child. The first shot knocked him back the second shot lifted him into the air. The third shot put him down and the body fluids came out. The GI just simply got up and walked away."

Here is an account of what happened to a party of Cheyenne at Sand Creek, Colorado, in November 1864. The eyewitness is Robert Bent, the half-Cheyenne son of a local trader:

"I saw five squaws under a bank. When the troops came up to them they ran out and showed their persons to let the soldiers know they were squaws and begged for mercy but the soldiers shot them all. I saw one squaw lying on a bank whose leg had been broken by a shell. A soldier came up to her with drawn saber. She raised her arm to protect herself when he struck, breaking her arm; she rolled over and raised her other arm when he struck breaking it . . . Some thirty or forty squaws, collected in a hole for protection, sent out a little girl about six years old with a white flag on a stick. She was shot and killed. I saw one squaw cut open with an unborn child lying by her side. I saw a little girl who had been hid in the sand. Two soldiers drew their pistols and shot her, and then pulled her out of the sand by the arm."

Former Army Private Paul Meadlo gave CBS this description of some of the events at Pinkville: ". . . we had about seven or eight people . . .

somebody . . . told us to bring them over to the ravine. They had about seventy, seventy-five people all gathered up. So we threw ours in with them . . . he [another soldier] started pushing them off and started shooting . . . off into the ravine . . . we started shooting them . . . just started using automatics on them. Men, women, and children. And babies. And so we started shooting them . . ."

The following description of the massacre of the Oglala Sioux at Wounded Knee, South Dakota, on December 29, 1890, is to be found in *The Long Death* (Ralph K. Andrist, Collier Books):

"The Seventh Cavalry . . . ceased to be a military unit and became a mass of infuriated men intent only on butchery. Women and children attempted to escape by running up the dry ravine but were pursued and slaughtered . . . by hundreds of maddened soldiers, while shells from the Hotchkiss guns . . . continued to burst among them . . . nothing Indian that lived was safe; the four-year-old son of Yellow Bird, the medicine man, was playing with his pony when the shooting began. 'My father ran and fell down and the blood came out of his mouth.' he said, 'and then a soldier put his gun to my white pony's nose and shot him . . .' "

Pinkville, then, is not an isolated incident in American history. The red men on this rock of an island know that. "Still, these things can happen in any war—that's the way war is." This is the statement which is on everybody's lips but which does not answer the question of whether or not they can happen if the high command and the government doesn't want them to happen. The Army has no trouble having its other orders obeyed. Why should it have such difficulty getting soldiers to obey an order not to bayonet babies?

In the case of the Indians the answer to that

question is that the government's policy has been genocidal. Even today it appears that what the guns and sabers of the Seventh Cavalry couldn't complete in 1890 will now be brought about by plain starvation. How else can we explain that "At the Pine Ridge Reservation in South Dakota, the second largest in the nation, $8,040 a year is spent per family to help the Oglala Sioux Indians out of poverty. Yet the median income among these Indians is $1,910 per family. At last count there was nearly one bureaucrat for each and every family on the reservation." (*Our Brother's Keeper: The Indian in White America,* Edgar S. Cahn, editor, New Community Press.) And if that sounds like a Vietnamese detention camp for American-produced refugees, the coincidence is neither accidental nor hard to explain.

With the Indians and with the Vietnamese many people want to know if extermination is the government's policy. Senator McGovern brought it up when he asked what the difference is between killing the population of a village from twenty thousand feet in a B-52 bomber and putting a gun to the head of a baby and blowing his brains out. The difference is that in the latter case there can be none of this malarky about attacking only military targets. What the senator drew back from asking—maybe out of shame for the nation, maybe out of fear of criticism—is how can this *not* be government policy? Both with the Indians and the Vietnamese, high government officials exonerate themselves by saying they didn't know about these crimes. If they didn't know, if it had to be brought to their attention by the mass media they are aching to censor, then it is because they chose not to know. Deliberate ignorance.

Three years ago, long before Pinkville, at the court martial of Captain Howard Levy, his lawyers offered to introduce evidence alleging the

United States government was committing crimes against the Law of Nations as a matter of policy. That evidence included such things as the practice of shoving captives out of helicopters and other acts that have just now received wide publicity. At the time the Army said it was not interested if such acts were "isolated incidents." How many isolated incidents are required to show a pattern of intent that cannot be explained away by saying that some soldier or other was mad that day? The Army's position seems to be that only a document in which it is ordered to commit crimes against humanity constitutes proof that committing such crimes is policy. Even Hitler and Stalin wrote no such documents but dressed their murders up in evasive language wherein words like peace and freedom were frequently used.

The same men have been running the war since the beginning. If they didn't know these acts were being carried out, it is because they have countenanced and encouraged an information system that blocks out such information. Did they do what the king did with the killers of Thomas à Becket, what government officials have done so often, and that is say by winks, gestures, and nonverbal communication to their subordinates, "Do what you have to do, but I don't want to know about it"?

Maybe they didn't. Maybe they are just so slow in the head they didn't know what the rest of us have known for a long time; maybe they're so weak in command they can't discipline their Army. If that's the case we must fall back on the doctrine of collective guilt. A cop-out idea. Where there is much weeping and gnashing of teeth, and everybody is declared to be guilty, nobody is guilty and nobody has to take the responsibility.

Here on this island the red men know about these questions. One of them, a Blackfoot named

Lone Wolf, composed a song which isn't very good verse but it gets the point across:

> *Ah hai—Ah hai—Ah hai!*
>
> *Then white men plundered ov'r the land*
> *Buffalo bled, red rivers ran!*
>
> *Our brave men fought and then lay down*
> *To die on that cold and bloody ground!*
>
> *Our children ran, our women cried*
> *The deer, the bear, the people died!*
>
> *Ah hai—Ah hai—Ah hai!*

Right on, right on," the Black Panthers whispered to each other. The accent is on the second word of their street cry, greeting, and general exhortation which is usually shouted out. The atmosphere in the apartment was too concerned for that. There was fear there might be another police attack.

The police had attacked the party's local headquarters in the Fillmore District of San Francisco a few days before. The Panthers, on orders from national headquarters across the Bay in Oakland, hadn't resisted, but the people in the community had gotten very angry and started to riot. It would have been worse, but some Panthers broke it up and got the people to go home.

So, D.C., who holds the rank of field marshal in the Panther organization, thought the police might try to justify their attack on the headquarters by picking a fight with the people in the apartment. If they came, D.C. said, they would fight, "because this is home. There isn't any other place we can go."

Home was stacked with ordnance. The young guard who admitted people to the apartment wore a pistol and a holster and was carrying an M-1. In the living room, there was what the layman took to be a 30-caliber machine gun ready to be used from the bay windows overlooking the street. A snub-muzzled, cannonish-looking thing stood in the corner near the hi-fi, and another pistol was on the coffee table. There was ammunition.

Mayor Joseph Alioto and the police department consider the Panthers murdering brigands. The chief Panther, Huey P. Newton, is currently pulling time for killing a police officer.

The Panthers feel about the mayor the way he does toward them. "The Panther party has had twenty funerals since March 18, 1968. The Panther party didn't go downtown and attack the police station. One hundred and fifty of them came into the Fillmore and attacked us," said D.C.

D.C., whose full name is Don Cox, is thirty-three years old and until recently was a production manager for a graphic arts firm. He was living an ordinary middle-class life with his wife, daughter, and son. "Before I quit my job last May," he said, "I used to relate to antiques and Victorian architecture. I put in a lot of time restoring our house, but I found out everything I was after, after I got it, just didn't deal with the gnaw in me. I went on all sorts of trips just trying to get it together. As I began to check myself out, I saw it was this social and political system. The program had me related to all sorts of things that had nothing to do with me as a human being. Then one day I walked into work—it was May 2, 1966—and there on the front page of the *San Francisco Chronicle* was some crazy niggers in the State Capitol with guns."

It was that episode in Sacramento that first

brought the Black Panther party national attention. It also helped D.C. "get it together" and
showed him the possibility of a different and
perilous vocation for a black man who can't
stand things as they are: "We recognize we're in
a dangerous business, but life is really a question
of choosing how you're going to die. Are you
going to die advancing society? Or are you going
to live a little longer being a slave and doing
what the Aliotos want? The only real survival is
having your ideas in line with the needs of society. When we study history, we learn the laws
governing society and apply them to our daily
work. We study other revolutionary people. We
know Chairman Mao has a saying that 'Capitalism will be replaced by socialism, because this is
a law independent of man's will.' We know that,
and we know that's true survival."

Little that D.C. says corresponds with the organization's reputation as insane, kill-whitey
maniacs: "Huey P. Newton was able to step forward and truly look at the needs and desires of
the black community and put that in a form of a
program, but it's really a universal program for
all people. We recognize this as a class struggle,
not a racial one. There's a Chinese group and a
Mexican group and a Puerto Rican group and
even a group of white hillbillies, as they call
them, that follows the teaching of Huey P. Newton. Somebody made a movie of them that will
blow your mind, with them all in Panther uniforms talking in their hillbilly language."

Seemingly, the Panthers are able to do what
the Black Muslims were doing a few years ago,
that is, recruit young men who would otherwise
lead demoralized, semi-criminal existences. The
Panthers put down drugs, booze, and personal
dissolution while giving people pride, purpose, and a structured way to live. The members are urged to memorize and study the "Eight
Points of Attention," the "Three Rules of Dis-

cipline," and the "Ten-Point October Platform."

Some of the members get into trouble and embarrass the organization, which seeks to be known as a group of revolutionaries, not robbers: "We had a purge of the membership. It's still in progress. Opportunistic elements have tried to exploit the party, but we never try to whitewash foolish acts, which is what the pigs do. When a Panther delivery truck was involved in a service station robbery, we didn't try to deny it."

D.C. is uncommunicative about party strength, but at a "Free Huey P. Newton Rally" the other day, it delivered about three thousand black people from the Bay area. It is picking up more support and good will by such activities as its free breakfast program for ghetto kids.

"You have a federal government that spends millions on a poverty program that gives people pamphlets about black capitalism. Then come the so-called hoodlums who feed the people breakfast," says D.C., who still appreciates that nothing the Panthers can do proselytizes as effectively as the President, the mayor, and the police department.

Indifference from the White House, vituperation from city hall, and arrogance from the police enhance the Panthers' recruiting power among the young who will march off to what must end in a new and worse tragedy, shouting, "Right on, right on."

Michael Tigar, the young law professor from the University of California, didn't meet with his Friday class to discuss the scheduled topic of "Repression in America." Instead, he was last

seen being hauled out of Judge Julius J. Hoffman's federal courtroom and taken off to jail. As
he vanished between a couple of U.S. marshals,
the tall man made the clenched-fist salute some
radical militants affect.

The second day of the Great Conspiracy Trial
was a day to turn a jurisprude into a red hot.
Two lawyers were in jail, two others were about
to be put in jail, and a fifth will have to finish out
the trial under a contempt citation. His punishment will be meted out later by the teeny judge,
who bounces up and down on his bench so that
he looks like a small girl in an oversized dress
playing in her father's chair.

Technically, Tigar, an expert on constitutional
law, and his three legal buddies were hired by
the eight who're accused of planning the Chicago
riots to argue pre-trial motions. The deal was that
they were to handle the pre-trial part of the defense and then leave while the other lawyers
took over during the weeks of argument. But one
of these three lawyers, Charles Garry, of San
Francisco, got sick and went to the hospital, so
he couldn't come. The defense wanted to wait
until he got better. The judge didn't.

Charlie isn't an ordinary lawyer. He looks like
Daniel Webster and he spouts off like him. He is
colorful, white, and the Black Panthers love him.
One of the defendants, Bobby Seale, is a Black
Panther who loves Charlie Garry and doesn't
want another lawyer. He is claiming that by going to trial without the attorney of his choice,
he's being deprived of his constitutional rights.

The judge wants him to waive his claim. In
return, the judge will let Mike Tigar out of jail.
The defense says this is blackmail which, strictly
speaking, is inaccurate. Judge Hoffman might be
more correctly accused of holding Tigar in prison
for ransom—the ransom being the withdrawal of
a constitutional point that would result in re-

versal on appeal of the conviction that almost everybody watching this trial believes is inevitable.

The judge is doing a frightening job on people's faith in the integrity of the federal courts.

Kids from half a dozen or more underground newspapers have wiggled their way into the back seats and are sucking in the whole show . . . the judge threatening people with the U.S. marshals, with contempt, smiling his sarcasms on the defense and making everyone feel it's dangerous to remain in the courtroom. The word is getting out to a million youngsters and, the next time some older person gives them a lecture on lawful procedures, you know what they're going to say.

The judge doesn't know. In the elevator on the way up to his courtroom after lunch, he could be overheard telling a couple of septuagenarian pals, "Now we're going to hear this wild man Weinglass."

"This wild man Weinglass" is Leonard I. Weinglass, a Newark lawyer who is the No. 2 defense counsel. Ten minutes after making his opinions known, the judge was presiding in the robes of neutrality while Weinglass was making his opening statement to the jury. Weinglass had hardly begun speaking when the government objected and was sustained. Then with increasing frequency Hoffman, acting more in the capacity of a hunter than a judge, began: "Please confine your remarks to what the evidence will show, not what the law is. I will do my best to explain that . . . I caution you again . . . I've cautioned you time and time again." After each cautioning, Weinglass tried to pick up the threads of his discourse when suddenly the judge half slipped and half jumped off his chair: "I'll sustain the objection."

The federal district attorney had not made an objection. The judge had jumped so fast he barely

had time to get on his feet. A minute later, Weinglass was formally told that he was guilty of
"contumacious conduct."

"If my right to speak is constricted we have no
defense," said the defeated Weinglass, whose
most egregious act of contempt seems to be that
he wears his hair in the long modern fashion.

Having disposed of the defense's opening
statement, the judge then asked, "Does any other
lawyer have a statement to make?" Bobby Seale
got up. The skinny Black Panther looked pretty
good for a man who's been through what he has
the last few weeks. According to a note he smug-
gled out of jail, he was yanked here from San
Francisco in an insane and exhausting six-day
car ride during which he was held incommuni-
cado while he was jailed in Reno, Salt Lake City,
Laramie, Wyoming, Hays, Kansas, Springfield
and St. Louis, Missouri.

"Just a minute, sir," the judge stopped Seale,
"who is your lawyer?"

"Charles R. Garry," said the Panther. So Hoffman wouldn't let him proceed, saying, "You are
not going to make an opening statement."

Such scenes are shaking up the lawyers. Even
the government prosecutors are beginning to
look embarrassed, grazing the ceiling with their
eyes. Certainly the prosecution is almost superfluous with the judge running the case. But maybe
they think like the defense attorneys, who see
what is happening as an assault on the essence
of their profession, on their vocational conviction that legal procedure does lead to justice.

The embittered realists react by hallucinating
theater-of-the-absurd endings to the trial. They
fantasize that after the judge has remanded all
the lawyers into the custody of the U.S. marshal,
and all the prosecutors, all the defendants, all the
jury, all the spectators, the little old man will
lean over his desk and say to the marshal, "Now,
sir, put yourself into your own custody," and

then he will be left alone in his courtroom flacking with his gavel.

Even some of the radicals—no matter what they say about the system—have a residual belief that at least in the federal courts you can get justice. But during one of the intermissions, Anita Hoffman, the wife of the Yippies' chief prestidigitator, said sadly to her husband Abbie, "I just realized we may have the people with us, we can have public opinion, but *they* control everything. *They* run the courts, *they* run the jail, *they* can do anything *they* want."

Abbie put his arms around his wife and hugged her and laughed. "No," he said. "You're wrong. We're gonna win. The jury is going to believe us, and Hoffman is our new Mayor Daley. We're going to organize America with him . . . anyway, the most he can give me anyway is ten years. When I get out, I won't be so old that I'm impotent."

With that, he gave her another hug.

No one at the Great Conspiracy Trial thinks of its outcome in terms of guilt or innocence. You are *for* the government or *for* the defendants. This is in the nature of political trials wherein the specific accusation is either so vague it defies definition or is a technicality that has nothing to do with the reasons for bringing the accused into the dock.

At ordinary trials people regard the acts the defendants are accused of as crimes. They buzz and speculate about guilt and innocence. They say, "I'm sure he did it," or "I know he's innocent but he'll never convince the jury." You don't get that here at the trial of the men who are accused of conspiring across state lines to cause the riot which was the 1968 Democratic Convention.

Guilty or not guilty is immaterial. If you're for the government, you believe these eight men should be in jail and this is a way of putting them there. If you're for the defendants, you don't believe there should be a trial. Or that maybe Johnson, Humphrey, McNamara, Westmoreland, and Daley ought to be the defendants.

Yet for all that, the forms of the law court endure. The color-coordinated United States marshals—matching ties, socks, and handkerchiefs —move about in impressive, tough neutrality. The judge gets irritated when he picks up on the defense lawyers' implying their clients are as good as convicted, and that they are here only to make a record for the appeals court.

The forms of the law courts have power over even sophisticated and radical spirits. Neither cynical knowledge of the world nor bleakly correct social analysis can eradicate the last hope that there is justice in these forms, that some day the jury may come into this depressingly modern courtroom of aluminum louvers and undecorated functional appurtenances, that they may come in and say, "Dammit, no!"

The defense feels the tug of this hope as much as the spectators. After all, the jury is there and listening. The eight defendants haven't simply been taken out and shot by the Green Berets or the CIA. There is a trial, there is a jury, there are these twelve people, sitting, listening. Every form must have some kind of function.

Whenever they can, the eight assert their faith in the jury, whom they talk about as surrogates for the whole people. Radicals must talk this way; whatever the radicalism, its advocates always say the people will vindicate them.

The defendants' faith in the jury is more than an ordinary generalization. They have faith in these twelve people as a jury, as an embodiment of an ancient form. Thus, whenever the jury comes into the courtroom, the defendants and their lawyers rise in respect. The government prosecutors have caught onto this, and now they also get to their feet when the jury enters or leaves.

Since the judge has sequestered the jury in hotel rooms, the defense worries that the extended isolation will turn the twelve against them. They don't like the idea that perhaps for several months the jurors will be dependent upon the federal marshals for their food, entertainment, fetching their clothes from home, everything. The defense wouldn't feel this way if it didn't retain some hope that the trial is not totally rigged.

Yet faith in the forms of law is greatly strained. The defense and millions of its adherents believe the forms have been weakened by corruption and manipulation in service to the policies of the government. Around here you will hear references to the Spock trial and the allegation that the Justice Department got the jury it wanted by doing a security check on some five thousand prospective jurors.

Thus when the prosecution announced that the families of two jurors had received threatening letters from somebody signing himself "The Black Panthers," there was suspicion. It was immediately thought, though mistakenly, that federal agents had sent the letters to the two jurors most sympathetic to the defense in order to get them bounced out of the trial and replaced by more satisfactorily docile alternates.

It was astonishing how quickly nonradical spectators accepted the possibility the government was indulging in the crudest kind of jury fixing. A few years ago the same people would have laughed.

Confidence in the forms of justice depends on a

minimal belief in the government's fidelity to its own rules. That confidence has been injured.

In the last ten years that belief has been betrayed too often. Go back to the missile crisis and remember the public relations man in the Pentagon asserting it's okay to lie in the public interest; go forward in time to the lies that were told Congress to get the Tonkin Gulf resolution. An extraordinary number of people now think the government is no more reluctant than the Mafia to win a case by threatening a juror.

The very witnesses the government has begun to put on the stand impeach it. We've had the first of what promises to be a long line of plainclothesmen, undercover agents, and FBI operatives. You can't sit in the courtroom without speculating on how many thousands of people are paid full- or part-time spies, political spies, dope spies, sex spies. A nation infiltrated not by foreign agents but by its own political antibodies, by a million sleazy, slightly tetched, functionally illiterate undercover men.

The Attorney General of the United States declares electronic voyeurism is necessary to the security of the state. Every day some new atrocity is alleged of the CIA, or another Black Panther headquarters is knocked over by the police and converted into an Algiers Motel. As these things happen more people conclude our justice is based on peeping toms, bullies, and blackmailers.

Whatever the constitutionality of Attorney General Mitchell standing tippy-toe on a chair and sneaking looks over the transom into the national bedroom, these practices are discrediting the forms of justice. They are also giving impetus to a movement that is destroying them, just as the lawnorder people say.

In the old days when the heat was on, deviant behavior went underground. This isn't happening now. People don't feel guilty about what they're doing and they're not humbled before the majesty of the law. The current response is to go above ground, to flout, to wave, to exhibit, to inundate the law by multiple public violations, by ridiculing it, by smashing its forms.

People loot stores while the television cameras photograph them; there are fag power riots in the streets of New York; it appears that thousands of young men successfully and nonchalantly defy the draft; sex, nudity, hairiness, and rock music are deliberately used to weaken every institution that people despair of controlling lawfully when they believe the law is a fraud.

This trial is breaking down the forms of justice. The prosecution is appalled by the defense's taking its case to the television audience. The daily luncheon press conference put on by the defendants and their friends has demolished the legitimacy of the proceedings. The dignity of the court would have suffered less had the Marx Brothers been let loose in it than it has from Abbie Hoffman's interpreting the court's business to the nation via the Cronkite show.

While hope in the jury remains, the court commands a vestigial respect, but how are these twelve people to penetrate their isolation, to see through the snide arguing of lawyers and understand that what the government is putting before them does not correspond with what happened in Chicago the summer before last?

For that, like the renewal of the anti-war fervor now, was too large to be encompassed by any conspiracy of eight men. ■■■■

The moratorium isn't a protest. It's an ultimatum by an enormous section of the population
laid down to its politicians. That ultimatum says
there is no time left. It says there's no more credibility gap because there's no more credibility.
It's an ultimatum that says either end the war
forthwith or we will stop it ourselves.

That's not what the politicians want to make
of this day. A man like Congressman Rogers
C. B. Morton, the Republican national chairman,
would have you believe, "I'm for the moratorium
as part of our right to assemble." That's not what
the moratorium is about. The right to petition a
government that rejects petitions before they're
laid before it is a sterile right. It's using the forms
of political process to frustrate their purpose.
It's a con, a fancy way of saying, "You go ahead
and exercise your god-given constitutional rights
to be ineffectual while we go ahead and run the
war."

Even before the McCarthy campaign, hope in
the right of petition died. On its better days the
government rejected politics with the contention
that the Rostows and Kissingers knew more and
knew better. They know nothing, but that's another story. On its worst and more ordinary days,
the government responded by tricks and falsifica-
tions. . . . Pull out three thousand men here, hide
them under palm trees there, don't bomb this but
bomb that, invent another round of fictitious
secret peace talks, run and cry on U Thant's
shoulder, get the Pope to hold your hand.

Now comes Senator Fred Harris, the Democratic chairman, saying, "It's time to take the
gloves off on the Vietnam war issue. It's nine
months since the President took office." It was
time to do that in Chicago, August 1968, when

the Senator and his friends kept the Democrats a war party and drove the Clean Gene kids and a lot of other people out of electoral politics. Today he wants to be a peacenik because he has a dawning fear that the people have had it up to their gezuk with this perpetual tragedy.

Every aspect of government, all three branches, have failed, but not all men in government. Former Senators Morse and Gruening are charter members of the opposition. Fulbright may have helped vote us into this war and into the set of policies which make such conflicts as inevitable as they are recurring, but he's said he was wrong, unthinking, and gulled. We must accept that. This is no longer a small protest movement, and it's bad to get into the silly, purist radical bag of refusing to associate with anybody whose anti-war credentials are dated after 1964. This war has taught all of us many awful things about ourselves and our country. It's not just Senator Fulbright who had to learn the hard way.

But if the few respectable men in high office could make such terrible mistakes, then the question is who should lead? Many speakers today will say the politicians, chastened, humbled, made honest and sensitive to the death of their constituents' sons and the voters' high taxes. Don't you believe it. Don't let them steal the movement away.

The strength of the peace movement is its leaderlessness, the way it can survive and grow on a consensual process which is as easy to see as it's hard to describe with exactitude. Let the movement continue to be led as it has, by its adherents, by small groups of people proposing an idea and testing it by seeing who and how many will come in with them on it. That's how this moratorium was started. Six months ago a few of the former McCarthy people anticipated that whoziz was as trustworthy as his predecessor when he said he had a plan for ending the war.

They judged that by October we would be ready for the moratorium. They were right. Today we put black crepe on our arms and refrain from work.

That will not be enough to end the war. We may get something out of it. Hershey's already been tossed to us, although what we're supposed to do with the old flesh trader is a puzzle. Maybe Hoover'll be given to us next, but these ancient bonbons have lost their sweetness. If we're very lucky, they'll give us some tinselly cease-fire while they sneak a secret war in Laos. The government should not be permitted to keep a single soldier in those parts, but to get them out we must do more than today.

In fact, today is a preparation for more. November the 15th is already being planned as a March on Washington. Today is a day of accustoming great numbers of people to the anxiety of standing up to their government. Even in a country like ours where there *are* civil liberties, great strain still attaches to exercising them. We were all brought up trusting the government; it's hard to shake off the feeling that resistance to it, especially about a war, is a form of social treason. The moratorium will make people comfortable in their new roles of resistance. It will make opposition socially acceptable, perhaps even stylish.

This isn't by design but is dictated by the probable course of events. Either the war must end or the resistance must grow and take tougher forms. The fact will not be clear in most of the talks given today because they'll be given by summer-soldier politicians who will want to felicitate everyone on their orderly, good conduct; they will praise their audiences for the lawful and constitutional manner by which they express their hatred of this lousy war. That's all right. Only imbeciles prefer street brawling and law-breaking to orderly political process, but that's not the point.

The point is that there would never have been a Peace Movement if it had remained law abiding in the government's eyes. The Peace Movement is where it is because people broke into draft boards and threw blood on the files or got their heads beaten standing in front of induction centers or, like Captain Howard Levy, took a court martial and a jail sentence.

They dramatized the war's nature. They forced the rest of us to go back over the record and check to be sure there was some plausible justification for taking human lives as we were doing. They did more. When they faced their judges and pleaded innocent by virtue of Nuremburg, they reminded us that we're individually responsible for what's done in our names. Our government, our armies, our taxes, our napalm, our soldiers, our young men.

These law-breakers planted in us the bad dream that there could be the Cincinnati War Crimes Trials of 1971 in which we would have to stand before the bar and plead we were good Americans. The Spocks, the Muhammad Alis, the Father Berrigans, the David Harrises, they did that to us, gave us the bad dream of the good American.

Their example shows that an action like the moratorium isn't an event in itself but the preparation and the threat of more and wider action. Even now what started out to be a sedate moratorium is inching in the direction of a general strike. It hasn't reached that point yet, but it will unless the government capitulates to its citizens.

But what's-his-face, the furtive and fugitive President who darts from TV station to armed compound, doesn't know that; he doesn't know that if he keeps it up, by spring the country may be ungovernable. He says he won't be the first American President to lose a war, when what he risks is becoming the first President to lose America.

Maybe today he will read the ultimatum correctly and understand that playtime is over. That there is no patience left for Henry Cabot Lodge, Ellsworth Bunker, and more diddlybop about bugging out, leaving allies in the lurch, or saving the State Department's occidental face. People don't care if we bug out, run out, march out, stumble out, crawl out, or fade out as long as we get out *now*. They've had it, and the tumult and anger is spreading everywhere. Even the federal bureaucracy is threatening to take to the streets. It's no longer students or blacks; it's older people, businessmen, conservatives, liberals, anti-Communists, pro-Communists; it's everybody who knows that a perennial war that we have no will to win or even fight is insanity, that a democracy which carries on a war that 40 or 50 per cent of the population detests risks destroying itself.   ■■■

After George Wald gave his speech at MIT, you encountered it everywhere. Copies of it were sent through the mail, passed from friend to friend. Large excerpts were printed in the *New Yorker* magazine, and the *Washington Post* printed the full text of what the Harvard Nobel Laureate in biology said.

There was little that was terribly new in it, but it has had a large and growing impact because it is a complete statement of those who love life and respect it. In George Wald's words, they recognized their own sad passion at the coming end of the human race.

He spoke for them when he said, ''A few

months ago Senator Richard Russell of Georgia ended a speech in the Senate with the words: 'If we have to start over again with another Adam and Eve, I want them to be Americans and I want them on this continent and not in Europe.' That was a United States Senator making a patriotic speech. Well, here is a Nobel Laureate who thinks that those words are criminally insane."

The Senator is a powerful old man, bequeathing a patrimony of annihilation while Wald pleads for us: "The thought that we're in competition with Russians or Chinese is all a mistake and trivial. Only mutual destruction lies that way. We are one species, with a world to win. There's life all over this universe, but we are the only men."

Now when we're taken up with debate over spending more millions to make race suicide more certain, some people ask how could we have done this to ourselves? The responses to that can be many and varied, but Wald supplied one when he said: "We are living in a world in which all wars are wars of defense. All war departments are now defense departments. This is all part of the double-talk of our time. The aggressor is always on the other side."

It took more than the technical ability to build the bombs and rockets to bring us to our present, miserable, cowering terror. We talked ourselves into it. We used words in such a way as to make madness appear rational. In this the mass media, especially newspapers and television, can take a goodly share of the blame.

The media's credulous acceptance of government officials' definitions has been remarked on often in the last years as it has been learned that trust and faith are virtues in religion but not in journalism. There is, however, a greater, if less obvious, media contribution to the destruction of the world which becomes evident when you

study many of the reports from Vietnam that
pass for unbiased journalism. It is a bias so pervasive that its practitioners are unaware of it. For
people sensitized to it it's blatant in almost every
war story which refers to the National Liberation
Front or the North Vietnamese as "Communists"
or "the reds." In itself there's nothing objection-
able about that. By most accounts they are Communists, or socialists, as Communists often prefer to be called.

The difficulty arises in our naming of ourselves. If they are Communists, then we should
call ourselves Capitalists, or whites, the naturally
opposite terms . . . like cowboys and Indians or
Israelis and Arabs. Using the ordinary rules for
"objective" journalism or common sense, it follows that if you denominate one side in a war by
its politico-economic structure, you do the same
with the other. Ah, but see what happens if we
do:

"Communist mortars attacked Saigon tonight
inflicting light damage in several parts of the
city. At dawn the Capitalists counterattacked
with battalion-sized infantry sweeps through the
rubber plantations."

Merely by matching apples with apples instead
of turnips, merely by using the word "Capitalists" instead of "the allies" or "the free-world
forces" or "our troops" or "the Americans,"
we've revealed something to ourselves about
how to look at the nature of this struggle. We've
suggested that the way we're used to doing it
isn't the only way. We've suggested that this
may not be a simple matter of one ideology,
namely communism, aggressively fighting nonideological, practical, peace-loving folks, namely
ourselves. We've suggested that, although the
mass media have taught us only bad people have
an ideology, we may also have one, that we may
also be a people who see reality through lenses

ground according to the prescriptions of political optometrists.

We always say we're fighting for "freedom," but so does the other side, the biggest difference apparently being that we are Capitalists and they are Communists. In fact, our disagreements over what the word freedom may be taken to mean arise out of the distinction in economic systems.

Unfortunately for people like Senator Russell and his fellow atomic nihilists, the general American commitment to freedom is much greater than it is to Capitalism, so that if the mass media were to fall into the habit of contrasting the reds with the whites a lot of people might say, "Hey, wait a minute. Is this Communist-Capitalist struggle worth it? Are we fighting for our liberty or somebody else's money?"

Ruling elites provide themselves with some security against their subordinate populations by encouraging the belief that all participate in the benefits of the society and the running of it. Everybody in Russia is a socialist, and if some are richer, more powerful, better-educated socialists than others, the distinctions aren't dwelt upon.

Here we do the same thing even when we are recognizing the fantastic discrepancies in wealth and power among our people. Hence we invent the term "black capitalism" in hopes that it will mollify the blacks, but at the same time it reinforces the doubtful idea that most whites are powerful, self-determining people.

But there are, after all, very few capitalists in America. Probably not much more than 2 per cent of the population could reasonably be called capitalists, and 2 per cent of the Russian population is usually said to rule it.

This opens the door to the natural speculation about why 98 per cent of the people in both countries should live in terror and die in misery to serve the misguided interests of the 2 per cent who will perish in the atomic day of judgment along with everybody else.

The mass media don't teach us to regard our own society the way they do Communist ones. As a result, we see ourselves as a happy and just unity in which all share equally in power and prosperity. We see the Russkies in an unjust police state presided over by a small group of tyrannical fanatics, a good people with a bad government. Their mass media do the same.

That is why all war departments are departments of defense, and the aggressor is always on the other side. Every day through every medium the people of each country are told they live in the good society, founded on the scientific understanding of man, a society frustrated in its desire to produce an elysium by those other totalitarians whose ideological perversions prevent them from seeing the difference between aggression and self-defense.

The mass media will either have to develop a higher level of self-awareness, a higher critical understanding of the information they put out, or they will assuredly talk us into the last detonation of doom.   ■

The fact of the matter is, most of us are broke. We go along absent-mindedly agreeing with the people who talk about the affluent society and tell us how rich we are. We put it out of our heads that we're broke and in debt. We turn away from the fact we must borrow to buy Christmas presents, borrow to go on vacation, borrow to put a roof over our heads. We hide from acknowledging that by the time we've paid for the car, the carpets, or the washing machine, they are old, used up, and worthless.

This is the way we live and this is the way we die. We have no capital resources. We pray for heart attacks that'll take us off quickly, because a lingering chronic decline is a financial disaster for the people who love us and must take care of us; the most frightening thing about cancer is the medical bills. We fear the penury of old age because when we are belted with retirement we'll be lucky to own our own home and have a pension large enough to pay taxes on it.

We preach free-enterprise capitalism. We believe in it, we give our lives in war for it, but the closest most of us come to profiting from it are a few miserable shares of stock in a company that doesn't pay large enough dividends to keep a small mouse in cheese. The truth is, most of us are job serfs. At a time when invested capital returns 20 to 30 per cent, we have no capital. We only have our wages and salaries, and a debt so high that something like twenty cents on every dollar we earn is spent to pay off what we owe.

Our insolvency is so discouraging that we lie to ourselves. We publish glorious figures on per capita family income but not on the ownership of wealth. You seldom read that less than 3 per cent of American families own 80 per cent of the capital and that another 8 per cent has title to virtually all the rest. It's too painful to be reminded that most of us have nothing but the job which they're always threatening to take away if we're tardy, impolite, old, sickly, or just don't fit in.

It follows that jobs—full employment—have become the most important concern of government in this capitalist society. All good things, it's believed, will come to pass if all the people have work. They will have money to buy goods and services which in turn will make more jobs and everything will be prosperously hunky-dory.

It hasn't worked that way, however. Although we spend immense amounts of money on job creation, the economist Lewis O. Kelso points out that, next to warfare, welfare is our fastest growing industry. And he's not counting our new, hidden welfare programs for the indigent, white, middle-class young—the educational dole which comes in the form of scholarships, fellowships, and academic stipends, all devices for feeding people while keeping them off the job market.

Each year the situation grows worse because, as Kelso says, labor—human workers, that is— becomes increasingly less important in manufacturing real wealth. We talk about the productivity of labor but it's the machines, ever more versatile and diligent, that do the work and make the profits, so that any system by which people are paid according to their labor is going to get into worse and worse trouble. Those who make the real money are the people who own the machines. Those who are paid only for their exertions must be paid less and less until finally they will be able to survive thanks to some kind of charity.

Kelso, an unorthodox lawyer-economist from San Francisco, argues that we would do better to forget about creating jobs and apply ourselves to making more capitalists. If everybody could own shares in wealth-producing machines and live off the profits they manufacture, we could abandon the practice of making people take employment which is either purposeless or actually destructive.

Kelso estimates that something over 26 million people are now hard at work doing nothing of any real value. He includes in this category munitions workers devoting themselves to overkill, that is, the manufacture of weapons in excess of what we need to defend ourselves; he puts on this list people employed in growing or manufacturing government-subsidized surpluses; hordes of union featherbedders, surplus military personnel, 3 million who administer welfare programs, and nobody knows exactly how many who work on tax-supported construction projects which have no other purpose than providing an excuse for handing out paychecks. This odd craziness is defended in the name of capitalism, free enterprise, and private property. Which is strange, since many of the practices necessary to maintain our bundle of economic contradictions are often associated with the most authoritarian and least successful socialist societies . . . confiscatory taxation, work without incentives, production without market or purpose.

Ordinarily the people who make a fuss over the situation are ultra right-wingers. But they're called idiots and ignored. They jump and they shout about the waste, and inflation, and the inefficiency, but they're treated like the nutty little man with the toothpick legs in the ad that says in Philadelphia almost everybody reads the *Bulletin*.

It used to be that full employment via deficit spending, arms production, and inflation was thought to be a Democratic party policy; it now arrives that the Republicans are also Keynesian in their thinking and only disagree with their political opponents over what's called "fine tuning," which is an argument not over whether we should have inflation but merely about how much is needed to keep our tipsy economic balance. It fell to this administration, which is advertised as illiberal and conservative, to propose the biggest, most expensive and most permanent of all welfare programs to date.

The result of this method of running the country is the progressive demoralization of everybody. As a nation we're like force-fed geese being stuffed with consumer items we don't like and can't pay for while we starve for what we want and need; as workers we're learning, to quote Kelso, "that the highest wages are not currently being paid for production but rather for being present at the scene of production as a member of a well-organized power bloc"; as citizens we're supposed to function as independent political beings when we're economic capons, near bankrupts, who're saved from foreclosure because our creditors know that we, the vast noncapitalist majority, have nothing but next week's paycheck.

Our government was founded on the supposition that its citizens would have property, real productive wealth; the Constitution assumes people with the vote will have a share in the nation—and not a psychological share, a nebulous sense of identification, but a palpable piece of the action. In place of this equity, there is enormous concentration of wealth among the shockingly rich, and, for the rest of us, flat wallets, insecurity, and a miasma of maladministered welfare programs that you wouldn't wish on a Marxist even . . . food programs that leave people hungry, housing programs that leave them out in the cold, health programs that put them in early graves.

We grow more unhappy and impotent. Demoralization and confusion eats into us. Being poor and without capital, we have only a peripheral place in the political process designed for propertied people. Without the power to exert real influence, we have also begun to distrust the government's ability to accomplish social objectives intelligently, quickly, or in a way that will leave us our dignity. That's why the varieties of socialism and corporate statism have little allure for us.

Now recently we've begun to doubt the capacity of privately held corporations to do what we expect of them. We feel this way partially because we've been left out in the cold without any share of the ownership, but also because we see them combining with government in those welfare/full employment/consumer endeavors. It seems to us that the big companies are sputtering and misfiring, that the demoralization is spreading. The phone company is having more trouble putting through a ten-cent call; General Motors can't seem to get the right nut on the right bolt; the wings fall off the airplanes. Everybody's going around telling everybody else, "Nothing works."

We need a new idea. Lewis Kelso has one. He's been writing about it for ten years, but we've been too preoccupied with war to listen. Now the objective situation and our own morale have slid so low that we owe it to ourselves to listen to how he would make us capitalists in this our nominally capitalistic land.　　　　　■■■

Drive down any highway and sooner or later you'll come to an automobile salesroom where credit will be extended so that you can drive out in a new, $4,000 Polluter 500, the hottest thing on the road. If you have any kind of a job, they'll give it to you for next to no money down. They don't even like it if you offer to pay cash.

The same thing holds true for TV sets, furniture, refrigerators, everything you use and want. There's a bank, a finance company, an insurance outfit panting to offer you credit at usurious rates of interest.

But what happens if you decide you don't want

a new, 1970 Polluter 500? What happens if, instead, you want to buy $4,000 worth of IBM shares on the same terms? You know, stock now, no money down, don't pay anything for three months. Blow that idea out of the other ear. Stockbrokers don't want you cluttering up their offices. They don't want little people bothering them. Too much paper work, not enough profit. They don't even want to do business with you on an all-cash basis. Buying a share of stock has been converted into an arcane, bureaucratic, and impossible process that most of us cannot participate in.

This is a strange policy for businessmen who like to brag about how tough and practical they are. They're willing to lend money, they're actually out in the streets begging people to borrow money to buy perishable junk, while at the same time they make it as tough as possible to borrow money to buy something of real value that doesn't depreciate faster than it can be paid off.

The Polluter 500'll lose a third of its value the minute you drive it out of the door. It's a dead-end machine; it's like an artillery shell, a product that can't create wealth. Unlike a lathe or a computer or a drill press, machines that make other machines and products, the Polluter 500 manufactures nothing but smog and congestion. Nevertheless, they'll lend as much money as you want to buy the brute, which is worthless as collateral, while making it as difficult as possible to buy a hunk of a computer which is the best possible collateral in the world.

This set of anomalous practices was accepted as normal, natural, and even desirable until they were examined by Louis O. Kelso, the San Francisco economist of no professional standing whatsoever—perhaps because his books aren't dismal and can be read and understood without a slide rule. (Highly recommended is *Two-Factor Theory: The Economics of Reality* with Patricia Hetter, Vintage paperback, $1.65.) While other economists play hinkie-dinkle with government deficits, interest rates, subsidies, and welfare programs, Kelso has come up with some new ideas.

He points out that all credit is made available to us on the strength of our jobs, but that human labor accounts for the smaller and diminishing proportion of the effort that goes into creating wealth. It's the machines that make the money. Consequently, the government must think up sillier and sillier jobs for people to do because their income is tied to the idea that you must have a job in order to get money, or, failing that, you must be on welfare like the black family on relief or Senator Eastland who gets his welfare money disguised as a cotton subsidy.

In either case, the money always comes in such a way that it must be spent on consumer items, on nonproductive machines like the Polluter 500. The result is constant inflation which is always threatening to get out of hand, but which we dare not stop for fear of a huge collapse.

None of this need be, Kelso argues, if people's income were tied to the profits created by wealth-producing machines. In other words, if we were all capitalists we'd have second incomes which would not be inflationary since they would not come from printing money but from the real profits manufactured by the machines which we own shares of.

But we're not capitalists, and that's the problem. Kelso says, "If we functionally define a capitalist household as one that receives at least half of the annual income it spends on consumption in the form of return on invested capital, less than 1 per cent of United States households are capitalists."

Kelso points out that 95 per cent of the money big corporations use to pay for buying new machines comes not from borrowing or selling new shares of stock but from holding back profits. Ordinarily this would be an outrage to their stockholders, but the tax laws are such they don't mind if they get low dividends. Mostly they are very rich and have other ways of getting their money from their stocks when they want it.

Kelso proposes certain changes in the tax laws that would compel big corporations to pay out all their profits to their stockholders. Thus when they wanted to buy new equipment to build a new factory they would have to borrow, and it's in this borrowing that Kelso hopes to make capitalists of us all.

Instead of going to a bank or an insurance company to get the money, under the Kelso system corporations would issue new stock which would be purchased by their employees and others. Where would people get the money to buy the stock? From the banks and insurance companies who'd continue to make their standard profit, but now they wouldn't be lending money on dubious collateral like the Polluter 500 but on blue-chip, absolutely sound stocks.

Assuming that the new capitalist decided to pay for $20,000 of stock by applying all dividends to his bank loan, he would, within five to seven years, have a "portfolio of diversified top-grade securities, capable on the average of yielding an income of about $80 per week or about $4,000 per year under current conditions." If this seems fantastic, remember that this is a normal before-tax income performance of a big American corporation.

Under this system the new capitalist would still have money to buy his Polluter 500 if he were so inclined, but he would have more than that. He would have a lessening dependence on his job and with that would come a lessening of the present irresistible political pressure to pay people wages out of all proportion to the productivity of their work with the irrational and inflationary results this entails. He would own a piece of the country in the same sense that the Rockefellers, the Kennedys, and the Harrimans now hog up great chunks of America. He'd no longer be a no-account, a propertyless super-numerary job serf; he'd have equity; he'd be a capitalist, too.

Such a program would be important for every-body, since most of us are broke and in debt, nomads in our own country, but it would be most important for black people and other minority groups.

There's been a lot of bilge about "Black Capi-talism," but when you examine the actuality you find it's a slogan—you see it's some pathetic, underfinanced, ghetto buttonhole factory, some misleading, insignificant showpiece being pro-moted by a flack from the Small Business Admin-istration, an organization that ought rightfully be called the Small Change Administration. You don't have to be Milton Friedman to know the big money and the big profits are in GM, RCA, and Sears, Roebuck. Kelso's proposals would provide an opportunity for all black people to get into that money.

He isn't going to solve all our problems. His proposals don't seem to have much to offer to help resolve the contradiction between undisci-plined, wild consumerism and universal, ecologi-cal death; undoubtedly, too, carrying them out will create new problems. But we desperately need new problems.

What makes his ideas appealing is that they'll liberate us from our old problems which are now exhausted as sources of creativity. Kelso's pro-posals do promise to free us from our morbid dependency on economic health through arma-ment manufacture; they promise a way out of the welfare mess, out of food-stamp plans and ship subsidies, out of perpetual inflation, and they suggest a means of doing these things that isn't too disruptive of wealth whereby 5 per cent of the population own the rest of us. He would do it without confiscation, without taking from the rich, or even diluting the value of what they own, without burdening us with a new, socialist administrative apparatus.

But if not Kelso, then something else, because a free people must own the nation they live in.   ■■■

We Americans are mixed up in so many killings, it's not easy to separate out the routine hits from the important ones. Anybody with half a brain, however, can see the offing of Fred Hampton, chairman of the Illinois Black Panther party, by the forces of lawnorder was the most significant rub-out of 1969, a year that made a late calendar effort to equal the carnage of 1968.

Until the gunsels gave it to Hampton in his bed, there had been two liberation movements in the black American world. There had been the one we liberal white people called "responsible" and "moderate" and the other which we spoke of as "militant," "radical," and "irresponsible." That's over.

Once Ralph David Abernathy wouldn't have been caught within miles of a Black Panther. But he went to Fred Hampton's funeral and spoke words of consolation over the man's body. Black Congressmen of the stripe who'd fidget and look quiet when Rap Brown's name came up are demanding the Great Panther Hunt be called off.

This is going to confuse white people who've been told that the Panther is a predatory carnivore in a land of herbivorous ungulates. To us whites, Panthers are gangsters, Communists, murderers, and racists; we believe Panthers are very dangerous people who must be disarmed immediately at all costs.

But the situation created by the latest shooting and killing in Chicago and Los Angeles is so bad we must make an effort to drop our ethnocentrism and try to imagine how a black person might look at what's happening. We look at each of these police attacks as a unique case, just as we look at Mylai as an "isolated incident." It doesn't occur to us that a black man might see a pattern in what's going on.

He will remember the Marcus Garvey liberation movement of the 1920's and the Black Muslim movement of the 1950's, both important and promising efforts at the political organization of the urban black poor by blacks themselves without hidden white financial support and control. Both movements were smashed by the white government.

We whites buy the Los Angeles police department's explanation of their attack on Panther headquarters on the grounds the Panthers in the apartment had guns and fought back. A black person might remember the infantry attack launched by the L.A.P.D. in 1965 against The Honorable Elijah Muhammad's temple there. The assault, also near dawn, included firing nobody knows how many rounds of machine gun ammunition into the place. When it was over no guns were found.

You don't have to be a fanatic or a Communist or an irresponsible militant to conclude that, if the police are going to attack you with machine guns when you're unarmed, you'd do as well to try to defend yourself. In fact, a nonwhite person might decide, after comparing Chicago with Los Angeles, that it was the guns that saved the people's lives.

Consider that in Chicago there is serious reason to doubt that Hampton was armed or ready to shoot back. (The police contend he was, but police testimony about killing black radicals ought not to be given too much weight.) So Hampton—possibly unarmed—may have been burst in on and slaughtered in his bed, while in Los Angeles, where the Panthers fought, that battle went on till daylight and enough people had gathered to see and be witnesses to any murdering of unarmed men.

Some people will read this and say the writer is encouraging people to pick up guns and shoot policemen. He is not. He is as absolutely against citizens murdering policemen as he is against policemen murdering citizens. It's wrong, unlawful, insane, and tragic. What we are discussing here is how it can come to pass that men would do such things.

We well-to-do white people, when we're in a serious jam, we get ourselves a lawyer, we go to court and we sue. Black people don't have money for that, and if they did, getting justice or protection from these white courts is a very iffy proposition. The white-controlled mechanisms of protection have been notably ineffective in keeping lower-class black leaders alive and well: Dr. Martin Luther King (murdered), Medgar Evers (murdered), Malcolm X (murdered), Eldridge Cleaver (exiled), Stokely Carmichael (exiled), Robert Williams (exiled, returned, and now jailed), Bobby Seale (jailed). The Panthers alone claim that twenty-eight of their top people have been murdered in the last couple of years, and there's no strong prima facie reason to disbelieve them, but these are the big famous names or the members of relatively large and well-known organizations. There are countless episodes of repression and violence that either go unreported or only get a couple of lines in the back of the paper. For example, in September 1969 in Camden, New Jersey, the cops raided a garment factory run by the Black People's Unity Movement, smashed their sewing machines, and put their leader in jail.

The best thing that could happen is that Attorney General Mitchell would get his mojo going and do what he's paid for instead of the opposite. Fat chance. So how are black politicals going to get protection? Perhaps the best thing would be for rich, white kids to bed down in every Panther apartment and headquarters so that the cops will have to shoot through them to get at the black cats. This was what was done in the South during the Civil Rights Movement era, and it unquestionably saved a lot of black lives. Even a cracker from the Justice Department is going to think a little before he messes with a young DuPont or Rockefeller.

If this killing and jailing and beating doesn't stop, the blacks are going to shoot back. If their lower-class political organizations are smashed, they'll do it under the guise of conventional crime. This is already happening. The urban crime that the government is unable to prevent is actually an individualized, unorganized form of guerrilla warfare conducted by people with little political consciousness but an overwhelming hatred for the circumstances under which they must live.

Hundreds of thousands of young black men are growing up in the cities without the Southern tradition of subservience which bred a self-hatred that caused black men to kill each other. They will fight lawnorder and they will be joined by a certain number of whites. The results will be catastrophic for everyone. Such will surely happen unless we white men learn that how we see ourselves isn't necessarily how we are. We've been told the truth about ourselves often enough, but we never listen. Nearly a hundred years ago, Sitting Bull, the great Indian chief, said it right and said it straight at the Powder River Council:

"Behold, my brothers, the spring has come; the earth has received the embraces of the sun and we shall soon see the results of that love.

"Every seed is awakened and so has all animal life. It is through this mysterious power that we too have our being, and therefore we yield to our neighbors, even our animal neighbors, the same right as ourselves, to inhabit this land.

"Yet, hear me, people, we have now to deal with another race—small and feeble when our fathers first met them but now great and overbearing. Strangely enough they have a mind to till the soil and the love of possession is a disease with them. These people have made many rules that the rich may break but the poor may not. They take tithes from the poor and weak to support the rich and those who rule. They claim this mother of ours, the earth, for their own and fence their neighbors away; they deface her with their buildings and their refuse. That nation is like a spring freshet that overruns its banks and destroys all who are in its path.

"We cannot dwell side by side. Only seven years ago we made a treaty by which we were assured that the buffalo country should be left to us forever. Now they threaten to take that away from us. My brothers, shall we submit or shall we say to them: 'First kill me before you take possession of my Fatherland...' " ▄▄

Harry Edwards is at Cornell finishing his Ph.D. in sociology, but he's still a marked man, a guy who you figure sooner or later will be put in the jailhouse or murdered.

If you've forgotten, Harry Edwards was the young man who raised a stink at San Jose State about how black students, particularly his fellow black athletes, were treated. From there he went on to lay siege to the New York Athletic Club and then really made it as an all-American villain by trying to organize a black boycott of the Olympics.

For this he got the same treatment given to Muhammad Ali, except that they didn't steal Harry Edwards' championship away from him because he wasn't a boxer but a track man and a basketball player. The sportswriters predictably castigated him. Even the humane Red Smith, who's as decent as he's gifted, wrote that Edwards was wrong for wanting to use the Olympics to dramatize black demands.

During the fight against the New York Athletic Club, and the successful boycott by black competitors of the Club's track meet at the new Madison Square Garden, Harry Edwards said many strong words. Some of his supporters were accused of intimidating people to make the boycott effective. There was some minor violence.

Soon this tall, extremely polite young man from East St. Louis, Illinois, was made into a "black militant" in the public mind. This is a fright word which turns off most white people's thinking values, so all they heard were some quotes about burning down or blowing up.

You can find out why Harry Edwards would want to mess up one of the year's biggest TV spectaculars by reading his book, *The Revolt of the Black Athlete*. In it he writes about the financial and political exploitation of black athletes, about the treatment of young men who are worth several million dollars in gate receipts to their colleges and about the way they are used by the government—for example, the State Department tours put on to give an idyllic picture of American race relations by presenting black athletes abroad. Or if you go to that wretched place he grew up in, you can get some idea of why he views the world so differently from the majority of his white fellow countrymen.

East St. Louis is a slummy concentration of railroad yards, shacks, gangster politics, a bad town for little black babies who're liable to be bitten by rats, as Harry Edwards points out. It's a place where the politicians and the gangsters and the crackers teach a strong, sensitive young man a decent respect for force, violence, and fraud, a place to nurture revolutionary pessimism in the young.

"I know," says Harry Edwards in his office in the sociology department of Cornell University, "I'm living in the most violent, the most oppressive country that has ever existed on the face of the earth, and there's no question in my mind if I continue what I'm doing and if I have any kind of impact, that this country, this system is going to attempt to move on me in some kind of way."

You can read those words as more militant raving, or you can try to see the world as life has taught Harry Edwards to see it. That's hard for most of us because we're so accustomed to orgies of self-congratulation about how great we are. We are always explaining how we are God's gift to mankind, how we are the freest, the most generous, the most peace-loving, the most altruistic human conglomerate that there has ever been. We believe all the wonderful, self-serving things we say on our own behalf, and if there are people in Hanoi or Peru who don't buy it, then the only explanation is that they are freedom-hating, war-loving aggressors from the dark side of the curtain that splits our mental and political world.

Harry Edwards is not our kind of political Manichaean. He was a little, ten-year-old boy when the Supreme Court said, "Let the schools be integrated," and now he's finishing up his doctorate and the Secretary of HEW is dipsydoodling over how to get just a few hundred schools integrated. So Harry Edwards doesn't see the United States as a land of peaceful change and progress.

He sees a country in which the men he admired most have been murdered, and, not unreasonably, he half expects to be murdered himself:

"This system has a tremendous capacity to wipe out the very individuals who could bail this damn system out. I don't care whether you're talking about Martin Luther King or Malcolm X or Bobby Kennedy or John Kennedy or Medgar Evers. Not that these cats were perfect. I considered the Bay of Pigs to be reactionary, counter-revolutionary and oppressive, but all of these individuals had parts of the puzzle. Nobody has the complete answer. The point is that if the system had functioned as it should, King and Malcolm and Bobby Kennedy wouldn't have been out there and they wouldn't have been killed."

Edwards has a collection of five hundred threatening, angry letters. They don't bother him, for, as he says, the one to watch out for is the character who doesn't write. This gunman doesn't bother him either. He continues to go around the country giving speeches and organizing black student groups while cultivating a certain kind of resignation inside himself.

"This simply means," he says of the possibility of being killed, "that whatever I want to do, I do now, because tomorrow I may not be here. That's why I never bite my tongue. To hell with the jail, to hell with the United States Congress and HUAC and the FBI, because they're going to wind up by getting me eventually. At the very most, I'm going to be able to buy some time—maybe."

The conviction that one of the many possible "theys" will get him doesn't depress Harry Edwards because:

"There's no question in my mind that when I go somebody else will pick up the gun. Malcolm went down and all of a sudden there's Stokely Carmichael and Rap Brown and Harry Edwards and Huey P. Newton and Eldridge Cleaver and a whole bunch of other dudes the press hasn't seized upon yet.

"The same system that generates and compulsively demands racists also generates and compulsively demands anti-racists and revolutionaries.

"And the next generation of students coming up! I was out in Cedar Rapids, Iowa. It was raining and snowing and this little sister was waiting for the light to cross the street. She was about six years old and this cop stopped his car. You know, a white cop who's gonna get out and show the little sister he's all right. So he gets out of his car and stops all the traffic and takes the little sister by the hand and brings her across the street, and this little sister looks back up at him and says, "Thanks a lot, Pig." ▬

Ambassador-napping is a new sport, another sign that as the leisure society spreads out from America and Western Europe, people everywhere are finding new games to play. Unlike many nonspectator, participant sports—shark-catching or lion-trapping, for instance—envoy-snatching requires little equipment.

You can get by and have loads of fun with but one dictator, an inexpensive set of secret police, a well-stocked concentration camp, and an American ambassador. You may have a little trouble with him because they're grave fellows, diplomats with initials instead of first names, and they're not used to having fun in the sun. As a group they're desk-bound, always reading cables and composing aides-memoires. It's hard for them to relax.

They played the game in Rio, but Ambassador C. Burke Elbrick didn't groove on it. He was a poor sport, and after the game was over he called the other players "young, intelligent, determined fanatics." The expression "sports fan" derives from the word fanatic, a name that grinds affix to anybody who likes to get out every so often and have a good time.

"I told them I deplored violence in any form," he said afterward in the locker room. The remark must have surprised his fellow players because it was the American who introduced to Latin America that most vigorous of contact sports, the game called "Marines," "CIA" or "Yankee, Go Home." The name varies depending on whether you're in Santo Domingo, Cuba, Nicaragua, Mexico, or Guatemala.

Stories out of Rio tell us the Ambassador is fearful that as a result of the game his usefulness there is at an end. It's true he didn't show the finesse we associate with his occupation. A diplomat is supposed to tell people how good their food tastes even when it's garbage; he's got to praise their art and their sports, too. The expression "diplomatically suave" derives from the word ambassador.

Instead, C. Burke Elbrick put his hosts down. He admits to saying "that their choice of life is not a very pleasant one and a risky one. I said there were other ways to achieve their objectives." If you're a citizen of a big, rich country like America where we spend millions of dollars every year on recreation, that may be true. But people who live in poverty-stricken little military dictatorships that have to scrimp by selling coffee beans and mineral rights have to satisfy themselves with simpler pleasures.

C. Burke Elbrick oughtn't to be so ethnocentric and snobbish. A humble man finds he can learn from the most backward of people. Didn't modern medicine get the miracle drug Alka-Seltzer from the Amazonian Indians who use it on their spear tips when they hunt the orange-festooned blah, that international pest which has ruined the social life of even highly developed countries?

The natives of Brazil are so simple and friendly they've forgiven C. Burke Elbrick. They want to steal him again and ransom back fifteen more. If this is done often enough and enough political prisoners are emancipated, he may become known as the Abraham Lincoln of Brazil. This is a distinction you get only if you liberate ten thousand martyrs, but with it comes a prize, an agreement by the government of Brazil to buy the battleship New Jersey, to be paid for by one billion square feet of natural gas or an equivalent amount of guano.

Despite C. Burke Elbrick's peevish reaction, envoy-snatching has aroused a lot of interest in countries all over the world where voters have defeated bond issues to build new baseball stadiums. Rumor has it that a group of athletic Athenians is making ready to steal Henry J. Tasca, the Ambassador-designate. There are so many people in concentration camps there that Greek society ladies are worried the new member of the diplomatic corps may not have a night free.

At first it was thought that Walter F. McConaughy, our man in Taiwan, would be stolen before the week was out. Later word from the Republic of China is that the political internees are either dead or have been incarcerated so long they've gotten used to their jails and lack the confidence to resume their former existences. In addition, Chinese who have great pride in their race prefer their own game. Mah-Jongg.

Iranian sportsmen would love to steal Douglas

McArthur II away for a set or two, but can't get a game going because of the inability of the promoters of the new sport to find anybody who isn't behind bars.

Walter Annenberg, the unloved Philadelphia millionaire whom whatzisname sent over to be Ambassador to the Court of St. James, is in imminent peril of being snatched by the Irish. The only thing that's holding the game up is a message from Her Britannic Majesty that if they steal him, they've got to keep him.

Because ambassador-napping is such a simple and inexpensive game, it's ideal for have-not nations, but there's a price for every pleasure. It costs a lot of money to feed, clothe, and water a diplomat even for a few days. Some of them, especially the ones addicted to golf, may behave like Ambassador Elbrick and refuse to take to the game. Yet even aging and out-of-shape ministers plenipotentiary ought to try. They will be richly rewarded. Not all of them will have the natural talent displayed by our boy in Rio; some may find they're traded for only a few raggedy guerrillas or possibly a couple of orphans suffering from beri-beri, but we Americans don't enter these international competitions just for the winning.

Like the Olympics, it's the game itself, the teamwork, the training in citizenship that will help an ambassador later on. These things are important as well as the fact that this is a unique opportunity for a diplomat to get out of the embassy compound and rub elbows with the common people—cultural exchange, that kind of thing. And for the home team, if they win they get their country back.

Mrs. Sarah Platt Decker, a turn-of-the-century women's leader, made it into the history books by telling the members of her sex that "Dante is dead. He has been dead for several centuries, and I think it is time that we dropped the study of his *Inferno* and turned our attention to our own."

The 8.5 million American women who take the pill must have been doing just that as a Senate committee heard testimony about the possibility that this drug may cause cancer. These were not the first revelations that the pill may have terrible side effects for a certain percentage of the women who use it. For at least five years, there have been low-key burblings that the pill may cause blood clots, stroke, and frigidity. Women have attributed a wide variety of symptoms to it among which are varicose veins, skin discoloration, hair loss, and emotional upset.

When you ask women if they reported these disturbing signs to their doctors, they often answer that their doctors told them to run along and not worry about it. This isn't so easy to do when the air is full of alarming news about the pill, but women, who're trained from early childhood to obedience, are frequently able to put their worries out of their minds and postpone thinking about this particular inferno.

From what we now know the only thing we can conclude is that it is too early to state with any assurance how safe or how dangerous the pill may be. This is a medical-research question which will have to wait on time, but there are other questions which can be brought up now and should have been brought up ten years ago.

Why was the pill distributed wholesale when

even less was known about its side effects than is known today? A lot of the answer has to do with the avarice of the drug manufacturers and their *de facto* ownership of the government agencies that are supposed to regulate them. The pill isn't the first recklessly marketed drug, but it would seem that in the case of a substance designed to be ingested by millions and millions of healthy people some special care would have been taken.

One of the reasons offered for treating people with drugs that may cause very bad reactions is that the side effects still aren't so bad as the disease. Undoubtedly there was enormous pressure from the people concerned about excess population to get this new and highly effective method of contraception into the widest possible use. Some of them may have felt that population control is so important that it was worth the risk of killing and sickening an unknown number of women.

This would be an indefensible position even if there were not other, and possibly safer, contraceptive methods available, but all arguments for killing and hurting people for a higher cause are suspect on their face. Maybe there are moments when such arguments have to be accepted, but never without debate and the utmost care. With the pill there was no debate of this sort; we were all told, men and women, that the pill was safe.

Another reason that the pill may have been passed out in such casually large numbers is that women were destined to take it. Any fair person who looks over the history of the pill's distribution and who knows the position women occupy in America must wonder if the same procedures would have been followed if it were a male contraceptive. There is no way to prove more care would have been exercised if men were supposed to take the pill, but medicine, like almost every other profession, is male dominated, and men do tend to take care of themselves first and best.

You can also speculate that if there were more women professionals more work might have been done on developing a male contraceptive, or, at least, more care might have been taken in distributing a drug meant for females only. We will never know, but the record of men's medical treatment of women isn't reassuring. You need only recall the hysterectomy vogue and the countless number of women who had their insides cut out for reasons that many doctors now think were too tenuous to justify major surgery.

In the case of oral contraceptives the same treatment of women as cheap and expendable appears to have been at work. In his book *The Pill* (Fawcett, 1969, 75 cents), Morton Mintz writes, "For years it has been an open secret that in some family-planning clinics The Pill is handed out with little if any regard for the examinations, warnings, and follow-ups that are supposed to be rigidly observed. Last year a Public Health Service specialist acknowledged in an interview, 'It is common practice for a woman to be given a bag of Pills and told to come back in six months, and then not be seen for a year.' "

Mintz is writing about birth-control clinics for low-income people, but it would seem that middle-income women often get scarcely better treatment. While there are many conscientious doctors who prescribe the pill with great caution and insist on repeated visits by their patients, this is by no means always the case. In addition, an increasing number of school clinics are now prescribing it, probably under circumstances not much better than those obtaining in the low-income clinic.

On balance it appears hundreds of thousands of women have been given this drug without being told what's not yet known about it and often with assurances of safety which the evidence does not justify. This has driven Dr. Herbert Ratner, the medical writer, into writing that ". . . Plato distinguishes between the physician who takes care of slaves, and the one who takes care of freemen. Whereas the slave doctor prescribed 'as if he had exact knowledge' and gave orders 'like a tyrant,' the doctor of freemen went 'into the nature of the disorder,' entered 'into discourse with the patient and his friends,' and would not 'prescribe for him until he had first convinced him.' The reader can determine for himself whether the American woman, as patient, is treated as slave or free person."

The Senate Committee looking into the pill didn't try to link it up with the state of women, even though this element plays as large a part in the controversy as the pill itself. Six members of the Women's Liberation Front interrupted the hearings to complain that there were no women witnesses or senators taking part in the inquiry. "Nothing," said one of them, "makes the oppression of women more obvious than the hearing today."

It may have made it obvious to her, but it doesn't to most men. In strictly masculine company, it's still almost impossible to bring up the topic of the treatment of women without being regarded as a kook. Men, especially in executive positions, will not even admit it is an issue, which isn't surprising in a sex that continues to believe it has a right to direct the most intimate functions of the other sex's body. Would we have the problem of the pill or all this fuss and claptrap over abortions if it were men who got pregnant? ▬

Not everybody who's insisting that oral contraceptives are perfectly safe does so because he's got stock in the drug companies. Many people are alarmed that if the pill goes, so does our best chance for population limitation. That would be serious, serious enough to consider urging women to take the drug even at the peril of their health.

The pill, however, gets the credit and the blame for much that it only has a formal connection with. This is the case with the sexual revolution which is supposed to have conquered the country and is now thought to be attacking the foundations of the American family. It's true enough that the pill permits spontaneous sex without worry about pregnancy. Everybody likes the idea of being able to make love without having to break off in the middle to fiddle with some sort of contraceptive device.

But this is a technical improvement on past methods and can only be regarded as the basis for something as sweeping as a sexual revolution if you take the position that what keeps people from each other is the fear of babies. Even unregenerate Baptist ministers don't say that.

Hard evidence about sexual behavior is scarce; statistics in this area are vulnerable to attack, but the weight of the evidence is that the true sexual revolution took place in the 1920's. Thus a 1938 study shows that about 75 per cent of the women born before the turn of the century were virgin on their marriage day, while only about 30 per cent of them born after 1910 had never slept with a man. Other studies indicate approximately the same thing. It was grandmother who was the first hippy, although she was called a flapper, and she didn't dream of having something as convenient as the pill.

The last ten or fifteen years have seen important changes in our handling of sex, but most of them involve a working out, an elaborating and proclaiming of ideas that saw their first acceptance fifty years ago. The reminiscences of Katherine Anne Porter testify to this:

"Times do change and vocabularies change, too, but in *my* time there was among certain advanced spirits a determined effort to identify—or at least confuse—sex with love; that is, to disprove the old theological doctrine that sex took place entirely below the belt and love entirely above it . . . the young pioneers set out to disprove this dirty doctrine in two different directions, or schools: First, the most popular, that sex is *all,* just plain undiluted by any piffling notions about spiritual overtones, or even just romantic glow—a good hearty low roll in the hay without getting 'involved' was the best, perhaps the only purifying thing in life. The extremists went so far as to say, and claim, they practiced wallows only with total strangers, so that no slag of personal attachment could get into the pure gold of sex. Hence a lot of young women taking up with Italian bootleggers and Brooklyn gangsters and getting smacked in the eye more than once . . .

"The second school still believed in love . . . Some of these fanatics actually waited until they were married to sleep together, but this was considered very dangerous, because sometimes, when everything else was perfect, sex, the louse, would be tried and found wanting. It was, therefore, much more sensible to have a few rehearsals beforehand." (From "Letters to My Nephew," as quoted in *Natural Enemies???, Youth and the Clash of Generations,* edited by Alexander Klein, Lippincott, 1969, $8.95.)

Whatever may have been the determinants of

sexual behavior for Katherine Anne Porter's generation (she was born in 1894), they included more than the availability of contraceptive devices. The same holds true for the decision to have children. The 1930's and early forties saw a sharp pre-pill dip in the birthrates. Presumably the Depression convinced people to forgo or postpone having children. It seems to have been more the latter since they began having them in unbelievable numbers as soon as the war was over and there was some reason to believe that prosperity would be around for awhile.

The baby boomers of the Eisenhower decade didn't allow their parents' sexual revolution to inhibit production of this oh-so-numerous generation whose massive size plagues them and their elders. The kind of open, experimental attitude that Miss Porter describes, that sort of happy, random, intense sexual life disappeared from public view to be replaced by the constricted do-it-yourself baby manufacturing unit of the 1950's, but actual sexual practices didn't revert to those of Victorian times. Only the way people talked did.

In the fifties sex got dirtier again. There wasn't any less of it, but there was more going through the motions of propriety, more feigned shame at being found with unauthorized partners. We demonstrated that we could divide our sex lives so that we could continue grandma's and grandpa's revolution while maintaining high baby production in a solid family-life setting without ever talking about what appears in 1970 to be a painfully difficult contradiction. (Wife swapping was started in the fifties but publicized in the sixties.)

At the moment we associate the sexual revolution with the idea of low baby production, but the 1950's should teach us otherwise. As in the case of the pill, you can see that sexual activities outside the bungalow baby factory don't have a necessary relationship to birthrates.

The mix of motives that decides birthrates is
to be found in the family, in men and women
when they're acting the parts of husband and
wife. Here there are great obstacles to achieving
a spectacular lowering of the birthrate. Some re-
side in the man, whose desire to have children
often seems to be downrated, but the most serious impediment is Mrs. Wife and putative
mother. If she doesn't have kids what's she supposed to do? How's she supposed to think of herself as a worthwhile human being? Before marriage and outside of it, young women may enjoy
playing sexual revolutionary or they may not,
but the hugest majority still want to get married,
still believe a womanly woman is a female moon
revolving around a male planet, still find fulfill-
ment in their traditional role.

Some beliefs are very difficult to change.
They're learnt from infancy from the knees of
mothers who've lived by them and think they're
the right way to live. Regardless of the pill or
promiscuity, they're three centuries old and
show no signs of losing strength. They've sur-
vived wars, revolutions, and even have lived to
triumph over the feminist movement.

Women are less of a factor in managerial and
professional occupations today than they were
forty years ago. More women work, but they do
less important work; they're blocked off from advancing out of their filing, typing, and assembly-
line jobs. To break through to the interesting
work they must each be Jackie Robinsons. He
was able to open up baseball for all black men,
even mediocre talents, but that hasn't happened
with women. Each one must break the ice all
over again.

The situation is so retrogressive that William
L. O'Neill, the historian of American feminine
progress or the lack of it, writes, "With the death
of Eleanor Roosevelt, an entire generation of
brilliant women had passed away leaving no

heirs. Not that individual women failed to distinguish themselves in this period, but not one of them achieved the stature of the brilliant galaxy who made the American woman the envy of her sisters before World War I." (*Everyone Was Brave*, Quadrangle Books, 1969.)

Women have no alternatives to being wives/ mothers, and this counts for more in population limitation than the availability of the pill. However, since they've been reared to be so docile and to obey when the society yells at them, it's possible they can be coerced into staying at home, popping the pill, and babying their husbands who can serve as surrogate infants. Then you'll see a new set of devastating side effects from the pill—those that come from degeneration, a feeling of worthlessness, emotional deprivation, and useless boredom.

While it's true that our honored Vice-President only opens his mouth to change feet, we can learn from listening to him. Much of what he says is country-club locker-room guff—the cracks about the "Polacks" and the "Japs" are just so much crabgrass bigotry—but he treats of themes which should be pondered as well as ridiculed.

"The effete corps of impudent snobs" speech was interesting because it didn't depict the antiwar movement as subversive in the old Joe McCarthy sense. Agnew doesn't show himself as someone who sees spies under the bed. He isn't witchhunting, and the people who liken these statements to what happened twenty years ago make the same kind of error others make when they compare a withdrawal from Saigon to an Asian Munich.

Agnew draws a picture of himself as a man surrounded by an irrational mob. The members of this mob appear to him to carry placards reading, "FAGS FOR FREEDOM," "DEGENERATES FOR DEMOCRACY," "SISSIES FOR SOCIAL JUSTICE," "PANTYWAISTS FOR PRIORITIES," "LITERATES FOR LICENSE," "PANSIES FOR PEOPLE."

This must be a terrible experience for him, this feeling he obviously has that not Moscow, the capital of an evil yet manly ideology, but rather a horrible crowd of perverts are sexing up the society and destroying reason and order by the most revolting hedonism. You may shrug your shoulders at this and say, "Well, he's just exchanging red-baiting for fairy-baiting." But this is larger than the classic American male insecurity; it's more than the brutish pastime of getting drunk and going out to beat up on homosexuals in the Bohemian section of town.

Agnew isn't doing that. He isn't leading a mob. He's expressing a theme that horrifies and angers many conservative people who're threatened by the kinds of currents which *are* indisputably loose in our society. Recently Governor Ronald Reagan gave a talk in which he evinced even greater fright:

"With the increasing affluence and opulence the young men of Rome began avoiding military service. They found excuses to remain in the soft and sordid life of the city. They took to using cosmetics, wearing feminine-like hairdos and garments until it became difficult to tell the sexes apart."

Ancient Rome is to the fundamentalist in politics as Eden is to the fundamentalist in religion. Man was expelled from Eden, and Rome fell for the same reasons, the difference being that in the latter case it was a whole society that took a bite out of the apple.

So the governor says of Rome in another speech, "We know it started with a kind of pioneer heritage not unlike our own. Then it entered into its two centuries of greatness, reaching its height in the second of those two centuries, going into its decline and collapse in the third. However, signs of decay were becoming apparent in the latter years of that second century. We are approaching the end of our second century. It has been pointed out that the days of democracy are numbered once the belly takes command of the head. When the less affluent feel the urge to break a commandment and begin to covet that which their more affluent neighbors possess, they are tempted to use their votes to obtain instant satisfaction."

Forget the fact that his history is hopelessly cocked up. Treat what he has to say about Rome as an edifying myth which, like all such fairy tales, is supposed to tell us how to act now. The good society of good citizens is pious, manly in the military sense of the word, frugal, ferociously self-disciplined, and harshly puritan in its sexual behavior.

The internal man in such a society is well ordered and positively certain in his beliefs and his opinions; he is tight inside, unplayful, drastically limited in the pleasures he'll permit himself, and, above all, he—and it is a he, for this is a very man-dominated vision—wears a mask and a full set of clothes. The citizen of Roman Eden, the Reagan/Agnew ideal American, has a public face and personality which, as businessman/father/husband/voter or whatever, he wears over his private, personal, often agonized self. He is, par excellence, Un-Together Man.

The Reagans and the Agnews are now being assaulted by Together Man—as in the expression, "I'm getting myself together." By the old

Roman understanding, Together Man is a slob, and a dangerous one. He's a slob because he wears no mask and no suit of clothes. He gets himself together, both his public and private faces, which means he recognizes all his feelings, his needs, his drives, his fantastical ravings, his raveled and free-form thoughts, and none of this shames him.

This is one of the reasons nudity is so popular at the moment. This aspect of it has nothing to do with shocking stuffed shirts. People take off their clothes to get themselves together, to cast away the mask. This is also why unbelievably large numbers are into sensitivity training. Part of getting themselves together is learning how to feel and be felt, to come alive by recognizing the body and its capacities.

Together Man can live with disorder. When he does order thought, he does it differently from Un-Together Man, who confuses reason with a beaux arts formality. His is the open-minded, free-form, playful reason with strange, new logics which terrify people like Reagan, who say this of education and teachers:

"Among the teachers and scholars [of old Rome] there was a group called the Cynics who let their hair and beards grow, were slovenly in their dress, professing an indifference to worldly goods; and they heaped scorn on what they called the middle-class culture. . . . To discuss freely all sides of all questions without value is to ensure the creation of a generation of uninformed and talkative minds."

Un-Together Man shrieks at doubt. It is sloppy, it leads to beards, to the nudity of the inner, passionate person who once he has his clothes off will wiggle his pelvis, dance to West African rhythm, and go wild in the streets. Un-Together Man sees a straight line of causality from modern mathematics to De Kooning to Watts and Columbia.

All of this is made more painful and bitter because the Agnews and the Reagans know that these playful people who show off their bodies, do it in the road, and unashamedly delight in touching, smelling, and tasting are increasingly the prime creators and maintainers of our technology. Look who wears the bell-bottom pants in our national family.

Agnew and Reagan know who does and so they struggle and hit out, but they're unequipped. Together Man is so free-flowing that he won't stand still and fight: he won't stay in the political arena. Agnew and all those guys try to get him back into formal politics, but the line between politics and art, sex, music, and clothes has become a porous membrane. The Romans draw their swords and go through the membrane curtain to attack the effete and the hirsute, to restore the old categories, put them back on their pedestals like a row of Corinthian columns.

The battle is joined everywhere but not along class lines. Rich fight rich, poor fight poor, the middle splits. The fight is for the inner space of man, and it cannot be kept in courts or legislatures. It is fought in schools, barbershops, dress stores, music studios, suburbs. It will last a long time and will only end when the modern Romans go the way of the old.   ▬

It used to be that if you had a white-collar job, the absolutely worst thing that could happen was that your kid might call up and say, "Dad, I've only got one phone call so don't get mad and hang up, but I'm in jail."

It used to be that while that was the final disgrace—worse than welfare even—it never happened. White-collar people, young or old, were too well drilled to get arrested for anything more than speeding. Still, the horrible thought, the scandal of it, the possible loss of job or financial preferment, the social disapproval kept the idea as a vague, unformed fear in the back of the middle-class brain.

Even the law, merciless mechanism that it may be, took pity on middle-class man in this predicament and the names of juvenile defendants were kept secret. Yet middle-class papa and white-collar mama could never be sure those arrest records were not revealed. So they would shout and implore their young ones to remember "what it'll do to you if you ever want a job with the government or with a big corporation or if you ever need a security clearance. You'll ruin your future."

Now all of that is changing. Every day thousands of kids are being busted for pot, for the draft, for printing newspapers, for subversive hairstyles, for music, for being young in public. If the trend continues it will be the young person without a jail record who'll have some explaining to do. The new college graduate with a spotless arrest sheet may appear to the personnel manager of the mid-seventies as a maladjusted loner, a deviant who couldn't relate to his peer group, a person who's missed out on his generation's greatest formative experience—pulling time in some joint.

It may be that by the mid-seventies, discharge papers from jail will be as necessary for the young aspirant in life as discharge papers from the armed services were to his father. The penitentiary a person served in could be as important as the name of a man's college. For example, we could have the equivalent of Ivy League pens. Sing Sing may be the Harvard of the future; Leavenworth may be the new Yale.

The first generation of middle-class, professionally educated felons hasn't found prison particularly appealing. They're pioneers, however, like the first rich people to move into a quaint old slum neighborhood which is in the process of being fashionably restored. The first people have to put up with the poor and unhealthy for a while, with the petty street criminals, until the renewal program is well underway.

Even now, things aren't as bad as they might be. Really disreputable people are seldom found in prisons. With all the raging and carrying on about the Mafia, you have a better chance of winning the Irish Sweepstakes than meeting a member of this much-denounced organization in any penitentiary.

A lot of parents may not see it in this light. Prisons, probably through no fault of their own, have gotten a bad name. They're supposed to be places where the worst sort of people live—jackrollers, bank robbers, car stealers, and murderously jealous husbands. Naturally a concerned parent wouldn't want a child emulating such people.

However, the statistics show that most people in these blood-curdling occupations do not live in jails, and those who do have made precious little money from their work; they're scarcely successful enough to trap an intelligent young person into copying them. There's no use denying there is some risk that a person may come under evil influences in jail, but look what can happen if you send a boy to Princeton. He might learn how to drink or smoke dope or behave less than properly toward a girl.

A young man will escape all contact with these three evils if he's sent to any reasonably well-run place of incarceration. In jail he won't be allowed to see violent TV shows or sexy movies. He will also be kept away from people who might teach him how to commit such socially questionable acts as conflict of interest.

In prison, your son or daughter will not learn how to beat a conspiracy rap with a consent decree. This is how some of the automobile manufacturers got out of the accusation that they conspired to suppress the development and installation of anti-pollution devices on cars.

Nothing can be more damaging to a teen-ager without a fully matured moral sense than to meet and associate with a member of Congress. In prison your child will never meet a member of Congress, or an administrative assistant, or a campaign contributor, or a businessman who wants a Congressman to put in a good word with a regulatory agency. Such men are never known to violate the law.

When your child is older, he'll understand that there is nothing wrong with a man sitting in Congress and voting himself hundreds of thousands of dollars in subsidies or special tax concessions. A young person without experience in life has trouble distinguishing between a secret campaign contribution and a bribe, which is another reason why kids belong in jail.

Behind prison walls things are simpler. They won't have to worry themselves about cyclamate and who arranged it that this stuff could be sold to millions of people for years without anybody being positively sure it was safe. Behind bars they can drink their diet cola and not worry about what people are putting in the bread and the milk and the anti-perspirants.

Today's parent shouldn't think of the penitentiary as a place of shame but as a modern monastery where a young person is shielded from Washington law firms, from regulatory agencies, from selling secondhand guns out the back door of the Pentagon, from the cost overruns, from the delayed kickback (I do you a favor now when

I'm in government, you fix me up with a fat job later), from all the perfectly lawful operations which keep their perpetrators out of stir. The worst your boy's going to learn in jail is how to pick a lock or knock over a gas station; there are very few persons in jail for committing more than a couple of murders—what's the Boston Strangler got to boast about in comparison with men who legally can kill us by taking strength from our food, health from our water, and life from our air?

Many people misjudge jails. They think of them as they used to be, full of tough, unappetizing rowdies. Nowadays some of the most admirable people go to jail. The jails are full of our most respected priests, ministers, and rabbis, the very persons you want your children to be influenced by. Running around loose your boy might bump into somebody from John W. McCormack's office; in jail he might be lucky enough to share a cell with Father Berrigan. ▪▪▪

The Feds are accusing CBS' Chicago TV station (WBBM) of prearranging a pot party for a documentary. If the accusation is true—the network denies it—CBS had better get itself some new reporters. No journalist should have to set up a party as though it were some rare event. The stuff is everywhere.

Its use among people in all branches of the mass media has shot up in the last few years. In all likelihood, CBS could have made its documentary by filming some of its own staff turning on. It chose instead to film kids at Northwestern

University, thereby perpetuating the idea that marijuana use is limited to collegiate youth.

It is not. By every indication available in this murky area of our national life, pot smoking is now indulged in by a growing number of middle-class professionals, particularly in the thirty-to-forty age group. More and more people in relatively high levels of government and society appear to smoke it often. Use of the drug in the Armed Forces is also common.

The mass media response to marijuana has suffered from a good deal of wobble, ranging from the hysterical and the ignorant to well-researched offerings which have hinted at the advisability of lessening the penalties for using the stuff. The media, however, have not seriously discussed legalizing it.

The public is left with the impression that marijuana can be either entirely suppressed or confined to the shadowed margins of society. This isn't very probable.

The use of the hemp plant is ancient and persistent. Herodotus mentions it, and there is reason to believe it was used by the Chinese 3,500 years ago. It's smoked in many different parts of the world by all kinds of people, so that the track record suggests its going to be about as easy to get rid of as alcohol.

The people who want to continue trying to stamp it out argue that it's bad for you and that it will lead you to try addictive drugs like heroin. The hard evidence for these contentions is next to nonexistent. For that reason, the government has just contracted with the University of Mississippi to grow five or ten acres of pot for experimental purposes, but as of now the evidence that cigarettes are worse for you is more persuasive.

To some extent the question of marijuana's harmfulness is beside the point. In the end it will probably be shown that it is bad. We're finding out that everything but pure food which we stick inside ourselves is harmful junk.

Nevertheless, there is no consistent public policy about prohibiting the use of things that are bad for us, or alcohol and tobacco would have been the first to go, with the automobile next. The decision to put liquor salesmen in the chamber of commerce and pot salesmen in jail is irrationally arbitrary.

The pot question is only peripherally medical. If a large minority in a democratic state wants to live their lives in a certain way, is it wise to stop them by force?

An article in the *Georgia Law Review* feels there is a constitutional "right to get 'high.' " It says, "Insofar as the right to use a euphoriant creates no hazard to persons not willing participants to its ingestion, it would seem to be part of the absolute . . . right to individual freedom in the pursuit of happiness."

This opinion is part of a large and developing legal attack against marijuana laws, particularly as they apply to possession as opposed to selling. It shouldn't be long now before some judge or other declares the pot laws at least partially unconstitutional.

The race question should have taught us that court decisions can't replace affirmative legislative action. If the courts move to strike down the laws for possession while continuing to hold that selling is a felony, the result will be worse chaos than we have now.

And the situation now is wild enough.

The National Student Association reports that in 1967 in California alone there were 61,792 drug arrests, mostly for marijuana. The final 1968 figures are expected to go over the 100,000 mark.

Again and again we hear of the children of famous people being arrested. Police all over the country are raiding colleges and universities the way they used to hit speakeasies during The

Noble Experiment, and with about the same efficacy.

No one can guess the strain on police departments of attempting to enforce a law that millions are bound and determined to violate. As pot smoking increases among older professionals, so does the possibility of blackmail. We've seen this with sex laws that no longer reflect actual practice.

Blackmail for money is bad enough, but in Washington there is the possibility of blackmailing government people for classified information.

The net result is to put thousands of people outside the law and increase their animus toward the police. Many young people have taken their inability to get a hearing on the pot question as a sign of their essential powerlessness and this, in turn, has sometimes led them to criticize the society with cynicism, anger, and occasionally with downright paranoia.

Some believe pot is kept illegal because of the beer and liquor interests; others are convinced that it is all part of a plot by tobacco companies, while they get ready to monopolize the pot market.

It's widely believed by pot smokers that the slang names for various strains of pot have been quietly registered as trade marks by outfits like Liggett and Myers. (A check shows this isn't true.)

Meanwhile, the hundreds of underground newspapers around the country have taken to routinely reporting fluctuations in pot price and quality the way a metropolitan daily newspaper supplies information on the stock market. ◼

WELCOME, VISITORS, TO FAT CITY.
There is a large, pro-American, fifth-column population in Washington which will welcome you, feed you, and give you a place to sleep. You are not in totally hostile territory. But be careful. If you haven't got it completely together, stay indoors or go back home.

The masters of this city are old and crafty in the ways of power. They've ruled longer than you visitors have been alive. They've had visitors before—Martin Luther King, the Bonus Marchers, Coxey's Army—and they've outlasted them all, unmoved, unchanged, and unchanging. They know how to turn back and dissipate invasions from the United States of America.

Washington's first line of defense is its ability to inspire awe. The domed, colonnaded, and scrolled buildings, the marble boulevards, the parks and fountains humble a person and make him feel small and narrowly limited in life and power against the magic of the temples of government, against the pomp of imperial Disneyland. Every year massive invading armies come armed with their Instamatics and their flash cubes, shoot off their harmless weapons, plunder the souvenir shops, go on the rides, see real live senators snoozing at their desks, and are sent home happy and ignorant.

Washington's second line of defense is indifference. Washington will outwait you; Washington will vanish until you go away. It won't answer the phone or the door; everybody will be out of town; you will always be told you're in the wrong office and to go down the corridor. The Rev. Ralph Abernathy built Resurrection City and sat here for months, but it did no good. What is a year for a soldier in Vietnam or a mother

waiting for a welfare check is a minute here—
Washington can wait forever.

Guile, evasion, delay, tricks, entertainment,
and *trompe l'oeil* all failing, Washington will use
force. Believe that, and don't provoke them.
Don't make the mistake of saying, "They can't
be so stupid. They don't want *Pravda* printing
pictures of them smashing in the heads of their
own young people with the spire of the Washington Monument in the background."

The masters of this city aren't stupid. They
deal in realities, not public relations. If that
picture runs in *Pravda,* they don't mind. In fact,
if it serves as a warning to the young and the
peaceful in Russia not to start acting up, so much
the better. The political and corporate bureau-
crats of this world have instinctual ties of loyalty
that supersede ideology. Marshal Grechko, the
Russian minister of defense, will come to the aid
of Melvin Laird before he helps you. On the
scales of balance of power, Czechoslovakia is a
counterweight to Vietnam.

The city itself is misleading. If you browse outside the tourist belt you'll run into the black
slum, Washington's façade of poverty. The people who live in it are poor and powerless, but the
city is neither. It is fat and rich judged by the
standards of places you visitors come from.
Washington's poor are a stagnant, ignored minority encircled by unbelievable per capita
wealth.

Rich and splendid, Washington has nothing
of a wartime capital about it. No sense of drab-
ness or feeling that it might be in bad taste to
display and enjoy nonchalant luxury when
American soldiers are dying. The White House
sets the tone of silver and velvet, brocade and
satin, dinner jackets and footmen, ball gowns
and wine. Call it the spirit of San Clemente, the
decorum of mourning lasts only as long as the
red dot on the TV camera glows.

The city is bereft of a sense of fitness of things, of a knowledge of what is meet and becoming conduct. It has confused pomposity with dignity and cannot remember that once these buildings, smaller and less opulent, were guarded not by soldiers but by citizens' affections and reverence.

The war doesn't exist here. Except when the people occasionally intrude, Washington's daily life is given over to fighting about boodle. The liberal, nonideological political scientist Harold Lasswell inadvertently summed up Washington in his little Eisenhower era book, *Politics: Who Gets What, When, How.*

"The study of politics is the study of influence and the influential," he wrote. "The influential are those who get the most of what there is to get. Available values may be classified as deference, income, safety. Those who get the most are elite; the rest are mass." So, welcome, visiting mass to the city of the elite.

People in town for a couple of days may not be able to find the elite and could mistakenly end up gawking at some little Congressman who merely keeps his nose clean and does what he's told. To find the elite, use the phone book and look up the National Highway Users Conference, the National Association of Real Estate Boards, and the Pharmaceutical Manufacturers Association. Don't forget the clubs where the white, Anglo-Saxon male eliters forgather in strictest seclusion to arrange who gets what, when, and how while grumping at a world that is beginning to figure them out.

The elite will ignore you as much as it can. To its members you're cheeky brats. Your refusal to wait out the seniority system of decision-making irritates them. When they think about you, they get angry and shout that there'll be none of this damn permissiveness around here.

Obey the laws and don't take chances. No holding, please, or, if you must, no more than you can swallow fast. Don't oink at the police. You can legitimately demand politeness, restraint, and lawful conduct from a cop, but if you oink at him, you're asking him to be a saint. We owe the cop the same politeness, restraint, and lawful conduct we demand of him.

The general situation here in Washington is better than Chicago but not so good as Woodstock. This estimate comes from Wes Pomeroy, the ex-Justice Department man who was at Chicago and ran the police operation at Woodstock.

He says, "The decision-makers here see their constituency as the silent majority and they think the silent majority want them to take a hard line. The Washington police department is sophisticated, loose, experienced, and professional at handling large crowds. Chief Wilson is one of the best chiefs in the United States. It's just unfortunate he's not making the decisions.

"Some of the things that have been happening here happened in Chicago. You see pictures in the paper of policemen practicing riot formation, statements about how many troops are in reserve. It's like preparing for a heavyweight fight. You have to have these preparations, but it's very foolish to play these games in the papers. It isn't going to scare anybody but it's going to be taken as a challenge.

"The entire fiasco in Chicago was almost solely the responsibility of a stubborn, unwise Mayor Daley who emasculated his police command. I went there twice before the convention as a messenger from the Attorney General asking Daley to let somebody from the government negotiate with somebody from the Mobilization. He didn't hear the message. The one thing Mayor Daley said was that if the Justice Department really wanted to help they could let him know when those out-of-town agitators were coming in to Chicago so he could take care of them."

It's better here, Pomeroy says: "Everybody's

learned something. There isn't the runaway
anger and hysteria of Chicago."

But it's no Woodstock either: "Woodstock was
our turf and our issues, peace and music. For
months ahead, we built in internal controls that
would establish a cultural control. We had food,
lawyers, ministers, and doctors for the people.
Our policemen were peacekeepers. Nobody was
armed. I designed a special uniform for them,
bell-bottom trousers, T-shirts with a guitar and a
dove on the front and the word peace on the
back. What you try and do is create an environment where people will do what you want them
to do and they want to do."

So now you know, visitors.

Shalom.

In the *New York Times* there was a very large
picture of a moderately small teddy bear in an
advertisement for Georg Jensen, the expensive
Manhattan specialty store. The teddy bear had a
wistful expression in his eyes and on his stuffed
arm, fixed with a safety pin, was a black band of
mourning. The copy read, "Some toys hate war
. . . no toys teach you how to hate or kill. Not at
Georg Jensen they don't."

The teddy bear had his toes up and his heels
down, as though his feet were dug in. The teddy
bear was resisting.

Resistance has spread even to the stuffed toys
in the nursery. You can feel the stiffening refusal
to go along, the incipient spirit of sabotage, the
conversion of timidly daring thoughts into day-

light defiance. The resisters are coming among us.

Many of them were here for the march, and some of them took advantage of the chance of their being in one city to hold a meeting at St. Stephen and the Incarnation Church. There were 100 to 150 in the darkened church looking at eight who sat on a low platform in front of the altar. Light fell on the eight and on the large, wooden crucified Jesus who hung in the air over their heads.

The eight were "emerging," as they put it, to tell the others and the press about what they had done. Michael Donner, a twenty-two-year-old community organizer from a crumbly Mexican section of Chicago, introduced the others. Jane Kennedy, a forty-four-year-old woman who is the assistant director of nursing for research and studies at the University of Chicago Hospitals; a young teen-age married couple from Indianapolis; five others, mostly Roman Catholic and resisting.

"We are the 'Beaver Fifty Five,'" Michael Donner began reading from a statement. "We are single and married, workers and students, young and old. We started from different parts of the country and ended up together in our actions, in our love, and in our responsibility—a community of active resistance. We claim responsibility for the actions against the Selective Service offices in Indianapolis on October 31 and the Dow Chemical Company in Midland, Michigan, on November 7.

"Some of us completely destroyed 1-A and 1-A delinquent draft files and ledger books in forty-four local boards in the Indianapolis metropolitan area. Some of us entered the Computation and Research Center of the Dow Chemical Company and destroyed magnetic tapes and processing cards used to store and process scientific research into such areas as nerve gases, napalm, defoliants, and other secret chemical weaponry. Technical marketing research information for these materials was also destroyed."

When he finished speaking, a young man with a yeasty brogue named Mike Cullen got up and introduced himself as a member of the Milwaukee Fourteen, another group that says it has destroyed draft records. "I'm proud to be here as a human being, not as an Irishman or as an intellectual. It's really a gasser," Mike said, more in poetry than precision. "Any institution of death has no right to exist . . . it's always papers, papers in files that are the instrument of death," he continued, trying to explain why most of the people in the room felt that these assaults on property were still in the nonviolent tradition.

Perhaps, but Irishmen aren't Quakers, and there is a determination about these resisters that's not militant but military. You could feel it when his talking words gave out and he fell to song. It's something to hear the revolutionary ballad "Kevin Barry" sung by an Irishman who means it. "Shoot me like an Irish soldier, don't hang me like a dog, for I fought for Ireland's freedom on a dark September morn," goes the chorus, and when he sang it each time, the people in the church would rise to their feet and silently make the clenched fist.

This is very heavy, very illegal stuff. It is resistance and resistance growing bolder. Calling a press conference to lay proud claim to such acts, that's bold. They did it to use the press as a means of telling people what they were doing and recruiting more into their work.

This puts us of the press in a tight position. We should not be anybody's organ to play music on, but these assaults are growing. A couple of years ago, a Molotov cocktail tossed at the Berkeley draft board was a piece of insane uniqueness, but now, in addition to the Catonsville Nine, the

Chicago Fifteen, the New York Eight, the Baltimore Four, the Boston Eight, and the D.C. Nine,
we're getting bombings and who knows what
else.

The media with no little reason have been reluctant to advertise and glamorize these acts, so
we don't know much about them except that they
appear to grow in volume even without publicity.
People are talking about dynamite, people who
never did think that way in the past, so we're
obliged to look at resistance in all its forms.

Another form it's taking is in the military. Anybody wandering around Washington during the
march couldn't help but be struck by the number
of soldiers—National Guardsmen presumably—
who were flashing the V at the demonstrators.
Other signs ought to be noted: a soldier with an
anti-war button under his uniform lapel; another
soldier inside the Department of Commerce,
which he was apparently guarding, with his own,
homemade "PEACE NOW" sign in a window.

A true resister won't ever give up. You have to
shoot him to stop him. Dr. Howard Levy, the
Army captain who was court martialed and sent
to Leavenworth, never ceased resisting. "I tell
soldiers that being in Leavenworth is no joy, but
then again, neither is being in Vietnam. You can
live through a stay at Leavenworth. It isn't that
horrendous. You do it by political organizing,"
says Levy. "The key is to resist. You can resist
in one of two ways. You can resist overtly or you
can resist by educating yourself. Eldridge
Cleaver said prison creates great poets or great
revolutionists. For myself I can tell you my
poetry didn't improve a damn after twenty-four
months in jail."

Now that he's out, Levy's still resisting by
working with the GI coffee-house movement.
There are currently six of these houses next to
bases where soldiers can come to learn peace
and radicalism. Three more will be opened soon,

according to the doctor, who goes from base to base criss-crossing the country working with soldiers who're resisting, organizing, and radicalizing from within. Remember that several years ago some of the most left groups switched tactics and began accepting induction into the Army as a means of penetrating and overthrowing it.

"We're still quite a way from insurrection, but you have to realize that if 10 per cent of GI's oppose the war in Vietnam in an organized fashion, the Army's in trouble; it's not like a college community where you need 90 or 100 per cent of the college students for effective action," says Levy. "The longer the war goes on, the closer we're going to come to that percentage.

"Most GI's do oppose the war. The Army is relying on intimidation and threat to quell attempts at organization, but gradually we're eroding away that fear, through the courts, the underground newspapers, the coffee houses, through rallies, and just by showing a GI he can stand up for his beliefs and his rights.

"I think the morale in the United States Army is at an all-time low. I've spoken to people who've recently come back from Vietnam and they say that if a man is asked to guard a six-hundred-foot perimeter he may go out sixty feet. The morale can be described by one word—lethargy. If we can increase lethargy, or if the GI's can increase lethargy, we'll bring an end to the war. Even Richard Nixon knows that you can't win a war without an army."

The government denies all these claims, but how does the government know? Does it have the information to tell it if a National Guard unit has become politically unreliable? Can it be sure the MP's will tear gas the next army base demonstration? Howard Levy says his side is making inroads into MP formations.

You can't take a Gallup poll on something like this. You'll only know for sure that a company or a battalion has switched over to the peace demonstrators if and when it happens. They're not going to tell ahead of time, because they probably don't know themselves. When such things happen—and they are very rare in history—they frequently happen not out of prior arrangement but because of a spontaneous act.

What we know for sure is that with all the talk about the government not permitting policy to be made in the streets, it's the streets that have the initiative. The resisters are out in public and audacious while in the White House they riffle through and count their telegrams of support when not abstracted by faith-healing and football.

Miss Doris Anderson is a thin, prim, black lady of thirty-five. She talks quietly and suggests by her mannerisms that she is one of society's mice, a scared person who knows how easily an inattentive hoof can come down on her backbone and break it—a small mouse who runs along the base of walls and only rests to look around in shadowy corners where with luck she'll not be noticed.

Even the prim and the tame, the rule-obeying and the inconspicuous have needs which must drive them out into the dangerously open ground. That's how it happened that Miss Anderson was trapped, caught, and put away.

She had gone to her social agency, the Baltimore Department of Social Service, because she'd fallen behind in her rent and the landlord had given her a five-day eviction notice. "I never

did this before—fall behind—for I've always
paid the rent, but I needed these things."

Whatever they were she must have needed
them badly, because everything about Miss Anderson is neat and planned and organized—the
way she has everything in her purse where she
can get at it, her going to school: "I'm interested
in data process but they don't have the machines
so they can't offer it. This year I'm taking key-
punching." You can imagine her going to school
for the rest of her life and their never having the
right courses, but she'll take them, do exactly
what they say, and nothing will work out.

Her worker naturally said there was nothing
he could do and sent her, as is the inviolate cus-
tom with social agencies, to another office where
Miss Anderson was of course told nothing could
be done and that she should go back to the first
office. Returning to the first office she asked to
see her worker again and was told by the receptionist to wait. It was growing late, the office
would close soon, and Miss Anderson, the fear
of the eviction notice driving through her cautious ways, moved out into the open.

"I asked to see my worker again, but the receptionist told me, 'It's none of my business if your
worker sees you. I've done all I can do. I told him
you were waiting.' Finally I walked behind a curtain in back of the receptionist where I saw all
these people at desks working. A guard with a
stick came up to me and says please for me to
leave. I told him I was sent by the man in the
other building to see my worker. He said he
didn't know anything about that, that he was
there to keep the peace. Then another guard
came in and started in on me. There was a lot of
confusion. I said I wanted to see my worker and
finally the worker came. I asked him, 'Why
didn't you see me?'

"Meanwhile the second guard said I was too
smart and called the police. They came and took

me away. They didn't touch me. They were nice. They asked each other, 'What are we going to charge this woman with?' "

Miss Anderson was fingerprinted and mugshot and put in a cell where she was kept overnight. In the morning she was brought before a municipal judge where she saw yesterday's tormentor, the guard who had called the police. "The guard said to the judge, 'The welfare department knows this woman is a mental case. She's a psycho.' Everybody laughed. I said, 'Who are you to say that? Are you a doctor? I'm not crazy. I'm not nuts,' but the judge said, 'You'll have to be evaluated,' " Miss Anderson recalls.

By now she'd been in jail all night and the better part of the day. She still had no lawyer, no clear notion what charges, if any, were pending against her; she'd been allowed no phone call so her family had no idea where she was; she'd been accused of the crime of insanity but had been given no opportunity to secure a doctor for her defense.

Back in jail her belt and any other object she might use to destroy herself were taken away while she awaited her medical examination. Miss Anderson remembers her examination by the doctors in these words: "I'm in the cell and these two doctors come. They look at me like I'm a pig. They don't treat pigs like that because they know pigs bring a good price on the market. 'Hi, girlie,' they say and let me know they're officially there to evaluate me. They ask me questions like do I hear things, do I see things, if my mother made me angry, would I take a gun and kill her? They asked me did I have all good dreams, I just told them everybody has had bad dreams sometimes. Then they went away saying, 'You'll be all right.'

"They came back in five minutes and said, we forgot to ask you a very important question. Have you ever been incarcerated? No. Have you ever been in a mental hospital? No. Have you ever been treated for anything? Yes, I said, I'm an out-patient at a psychiatric clinic. I asked if there was anything wrong but all they said was, 'See you later, Miss Anderson.' "

They never did, but shortly afterward a couple of attendants from Springfield State Hospital for the insane came and took Miss Anderson away.

The two doctors who examined her are paid $4 apiece for everyone they look at. They're elderly gentlemen, both over seventy; neither is a psychiatrist. Dr. Ogden, one of the two physicians, says he can't recall Miss Anderson's case, which isn't surprising since he and his partner see about ten patients a day by their estimate. The police estimate they see about fifteen, usually in about thirty minutes.

Dr. Ogden explains that no attempt is made to do a refined examination and that about all they look for is "exaggerated behavior." Miss Anderson says they never entered her cell but just looked at her through the bars. The doctor agrees such may have been the case, but, as he points out, at such wages you're not going to get a fully pedigreed shrink to get in his car and drive to two jails, men's and women's, every day of the week to make a thorough set of tests.

Although Miss Anderson wasn't violent and offered no resistance, she was put under restraints for transport to the insane asylum. "Please don't do this to me," I asked them, but they said, 'These are the rules and besides we have other people in the truck and this way we can be sure nobody's going to hurt anybody' . . ."

At the hospital Miss Anderson reports that she was given one three-minute physical examination and was seen only one time by a psychiatrist who said, " 'I don't think you should be here, I'm going to bring your case before the board,' but it never happened . . . If I was so bad I should have been treated by doctors, which I wasn't.

All I did was scrub floors and take care of the old people. That's what they call therapy."

Miss Anderson believes there are a lot of people in her insane asylum who're no more crazy than she is. "My God!" she says. "There're people who're just old, nothing wrong with them. One old lady said to me, 'You know why I'm going crazy? Because I've been in here three years, that's why.'"

The people who run the hospital apparently were reluctant to let Miss Anderson go. She recounts that they would keep asking her, "You're not married? You have no obligations? No children back home to go back and take care of?" They seemed to be trying to establish if she'd be missed in that outer world or whether they could keep her there as free labor.

After three weeks of involuntary servitude Miss Anderson was allowed to go back to the world of the living for Christmas holidays; she was told to return right after the new year under threat of being forcibly brought back. Luckily an OEO legal services office back in Baltimore had found out about her disappearance and incarceration. They got the psychiatrist who'd been treating her in the out-patient clinic to certify there was no medical reason for her to be behind bars, and she is now emancipated.

Nobody knows, however, how many other people are in the same predicament for as little reason. The Law Reform Unit, as the legal services program is called, now is in the process of suing everybody in sight so that the whole procedure by which Miss Anderson was put away will be declared illegal. That will do some good, but the underlying cause, the erection of institutions which treat people like baggage and make them live like mice, that can't be touched by a lawsuit.

The worst thing about what happened to Miss

Anderson is its accidental aspect. Nobody was out to get her; there's no evidence showing it was racial malice or a special grudge. She might have been a mother with a sick child or an old person whose children wanted to get rid of him. The whole business was so casual, so indifferent —the doctor couldn't remember her name. Aww, don't bother with her, arrest her, she's a nut, put her away.

Almost any criticism you want to make of OEO is probably correct, but one of the things it has done with its energetic young lawyers and its indiscriminately enthusiastic Vista Volunteers is that it has put people in these sad neighborhoods of American life who will bother to fish Miss Anderson out of the dungeon. This is no more than an act of mercy, but until the perpetually delayed hour of structural reform it is the best service that can be rendered.　　 ■■■

Why didn't NBC show the worms in the children's mouths? Wally Westfeldt, the executive producer of "The Huntley-Brinkley Report," says they discussed it while doing the story of the hungry, diseased children of Beaufort County, South Carolina, but the decision was not to let the audience see the parasites wiggling out of the noses and mouths of the little ones.

"If we have any value, it's showing things as they are. That's something a newspaper can't do —words can't convey a poor, hungry child," he observes. "But when we do show these things, many people feel we do it for sensationalism. We don't."

The networks are often accused of superficiality in their news coverage, so Westfeldt was bringing up these points during a conversation about NBC's efforts to get past the splash of the spot news story to depict the multiplex reality that turns ongoing events into occasional headlines. In the past, this isn't something TV has done either frequently or well.

That's why Westfeldt and some of his colleagues are particularly proud of what they did with the Beaufort story and the coal-mine accident at Farmington, West Virginia, that killed seventy-eight men. In addition to breaking the news from the site, H-B did four special reports on the black-lung disease and the miners' fight to get a law through the state legislature compensating them for this fatal disability, which is contracted by breathing coal dust in the tunnels. These reports ran a total of only fourteen minutes and nine seconds, but such is the power of television that Westfeldt has reason to believe that without NBC the new law would not have been passed.

"The story had tremendous impact in West Virginia. Fred Briggs, our correspondent in Farmington, says that the miners are convinced they couldn't have gotten the law through without us," reports Westfeldt, who adds that he hopes to do more of the same kind of thing. It won't be easy, even though both stories are specimens of conventional scandals conventionally exposed. Like catching a mayor with his hand in the city hall cash register, the stories represent a kind of noncontroversial crusading that newspapers like to think they do all the time, even though most of them don't.

The first problem facing TV newsmen is the public backlash arising from one of the medium's greatest strengths: its capacity to be exactly graphic, its ability to translate medical abstractions about infants suffering from intestinal parasites into the moving particularity of a worm crawling out of a child's nose. "Not long ago, I got a letter from a woman asking me if we have to show the horrible aspect of war," Westfeldt recalls. "I wrote her back and told her I know it must frighten children to see it and that it must cause them to start asking, 'Why, Mommy, why?' But that's what war is—it's people being chopped up."

That is what war is, but showing people being chopped up doesn't help to answer the question of "Why, Mommy, why?" This is TV's second problem with this kind of story: how to get across complicated analytical information, information which is as much part of reality as the moving picture showing what's happening.

The most effective of the Farmington reports was the one in which a doctor took a slick of black-lung tissue and crumbled it up with his fingers to demonstrate what coal dust does to the inside of your chest when you work in the mines. The program didn't go into why these miners have been dying this awful death for years and years. Where was their union? About the only reference to the United Mine Workers of America came when Briggs said that the union was against its members and "has been dragging its feet on black lung and mine safety just as much as the coal operators."

You'd have to look elsewhere for the answer to why the union should be doing such a thing. You could look in the March 31, 1969, issue of *Hard Times,* the Washington-based radical newsletter. It reported that the union and Consol, a coal-mining subsidiary company belonging to Continental Oil, "were recently tried and found guilty in federal court of conspiring together since 1950 to create a monopoly of the coal business for a few heavily mechanized giants." *Hard Times* has a circulation of four thousand, but if this news had been put out by H-B the folks in

West Virginia might have wanted to pass something more than a black-lung law.

Westfeldt answers that the reason NBC didn't go into these questions is that the medium is best suited for taking one, simple bite into an issue at a time, and that it intends to get its teeth into the union soon. The answer may also be that television news still lacks a tradition of investigative reporting. The networks have many superbly competent newsmen, but most of the time their assignments keep them too close to breaking news stories to give them time to go poking under the bushes.

Not that you'd have learned more about the coal mining situation from reading most newspapers. They have the investigatory tradition and little else. For a fraction of what it costs TV with its expensive camera crews, the daily press can look into these kinds of stories—but it rarely does.

As the black-lung story indicates, network news is getting better, but men like Westfeldt who are helping to make it better are going to be undermined if people don't get off the industry's back. It's already a scared industry and it's being pushed by Congress and other pressure groups into reverting toward being a sloppy, slappy-happy vacuity.

It's government chartered so it doesn't enjoy the complete first amendment protection newspapers do. Consequently it's relatively easy to push TV around. It fell all over itself trying to minimize its coverage of the street fighting at the Democratic National Convention.

Reuven Frank, the head of NBC News, wrote in *TV Guide*, "The time NBC devoted to direct network coverage of the convention totaled more than thirty-five hours. The time devoted to the pictures of the demonstrations was sixty-five minutes, less than 3 per cent of the total time." You will never live to see the editor of the *New*

York Times demonstrating his paper's worth by showing how a major story was downplayed, but the *Times* doesn't have to get permission to publish from a bunch of political slugs and Reuven Frank does.

Variety, the most important publication in show business, is writing about "a new age, a dark age of code office censorship," because NBC and ABC have agreed to submit their entertainment programs, although not their news, to an industry decency committee. This undignified arrangement which CBS had the fortitude to spurn comes from the mindless congressional yammering about sex and violence on the tube.

It will accomplish nothing more than preventing that nice Noxzema girl from kibitzing while our star athletes shave. On the other hand it will suffuse caution and timidity through organizations that don't exactly have a history of playing Crusader Rabbit. Eventually it may knock men like Westfeldt out of broadcasting. That will be too bad because the void will not be filled, least of all by the typical daily newspaper which has less than Mr. Frank's 3 per cent to brag about. ■■■

Y ou know what causes inflation?" the radio announcer on the ten-second spot asked. "Piggy people. So let's stop inflation. Let's all be a little less piggy. A message from the Advertising Council."

The Advertising Council has twenty-, thirty-, and sixty-second spots on the Piggy Wiggy series of business cycles. It has television spots that show people with pigheads and how they cause inflation. It has magazine and newspaper ads elucidating the piggistic teleology of cheap money. Deep thinkers who want to "find out more" are invited to "send for a free booklet" by writing to Inflation Can Be Stopped, P.O. Box 1900, Radio City Station, N.Y., N.Y. 10019.

And you really ought to send for one because they'll ship you back a comic book which begins as follows: "Jim and his wife, Sue, both worked hard, and, despite periods of unemployment were able to save some money.

"They had a savings account and a checking account and a few U.S. savings bonds in a safe deposit box . . . The trouble was, though, that often when they decided to buy something their money had shrunk!" Below there was a drawing of Jim and Sue with a balloon coming out of Jim's mouth saying, "Sympathy doesn't pay the grocer. What's the matter with the economy anyway?"

The comic book never answers that question. It never mentions the war, armament production, the moon doggle, the subsidies for business, federally supervised price-fixing, the fact that inflation isn't an accident but a government policy. It never suggests Jim and Sue are suckers to buy U.S. savings bonds, it never provides one bit of information that might help a person understand what's going on.

The piggy campaign is one of about twenty major campaigns put on every year by the Advertising Council, a nonprofit media-business-propaganda consortium founded during World War II to "put the skills and faculties of the advertising industry in the service of a nation at war."

It worked so nicely that after the Japanese surrender the Council continued and until 1968, the last year figures are available, it was responsible for a minimum of $338 million of free electronic and print advertising, plugging such things as savings bonds, Smokey the Bear, mental retardation programs, Radio Free Europe, Keep America Beautiful, Zip Code, the Urban Coalition's "Crisis in Our Cities," and God.

It helps but doesn't take full responsibility for such campaigns as the Heart Fund, Freedom's Roll Call, Big Brother Week, the Presidential Physical Fitness Awards, and the Annual Reporting of Addresses by Aliens.

Calling itself "the world's biggest advertiser," the Council estimates it has placed more than $4 billion in free advertising, and that figure is probably minimal because many TV and radio stations, magazines, newspapers, and billboard companies use the material without letting the New York headquarters know. No organization has more respectability. It has testimonials from the last six Presidents of the United States, and in due time it will get an imprimatur from this one—the Piggy Campaign was worked out in cooperation with the Nixon administration. Its board of directors includes the highest officers of almost every major mass medium and substantiates Vice-President Agnew's accusation of collusion in communication. However, since this single voice is at his disposal, he acted the ungrateful bounder in complaining about a few minor and inconsequential deviations.

The Council's slogan is "Advertising Contributed for the Public Good." And its definition of the public good is so accepted that TV and radio stations get brownie points for their FCC license renewals by running Council-approved spots. (There is no other way that a private organization can conduct a free, national advertising campaign of any real size, except through the Council.) So its idea of public good is of more than passing importance.

Things like Smokey the Bear, Zip Codes, income-tax instructions, can reasonably be called in the public interest; some campaigns are innocuous, if a little empty-headed—as the religion pluggers—"Live Your Faith—Light the World." How this serves the majority of the population that doesn't go to church would be difficult to say. Maybe this campaign is merely a clumsy and unworkable attempt at social control, but if the churches don't mind being brought down to the level of Billy Graham hucksterism—God as a member of the celebrity foursome on Bebe Rebozo's golf course—the rest of us are used to being social-pressured into looking pious while the announcer says, "Break the Hate Habit: Love Your Neighbor—Take Your Problems to Church."

Other campaigns which appear to be in the public interest grow suspect when you stop and think about them and who's connected with the Council. Every litter bit does prevent America from being beautiful, but it isn't picnic trash that's causing our worst trouble; it's big industry, a fact that isn't mentioned in ads. Since the Council's Industries Advisory Committee includes the presidents or board chairmen of U.S. Steel, Bethlehem Steel, Ford Motors, Aluminum Company of America, Scott Paper Company, and Union Carbide, it's to be expected that the pollution problem is defined as obscure, unnamed citizens throwing Kleenex out of car windows in national parks.

This is the same as telling people they're pigs to buy cars and TV's because they're causing inflation while omitting mention of Mr. Melvin Laird's rockets.

For years the Council has plugged the National Safety Council's line on automobile accidents, telling people that the carnage on the road is all owing to careless and drunken drivers. Undoubtedly these are the cause of many accidents, but

Ralph Nader demonstrated that many other accidents are caused by carelessly designed and badly manufactured automobiles.

Have you ever seen an ad on television urging the automobile and tire manufacturers to stop making unsafe products?

A strong case could be made that much of this advertising isn't *pro bono publico,* but is actually in the immediate economic interest of the individuals and corporations connected with the Council.

This reiterated national media blitz telling us that in dozens of crucial areas we small, relatively powerless individuals are to blame or must do something takes the heat off the big guys. This is even true of our beloved furry friend, Ole Smokey the Bear. Forest fires are a danger to our wildlife resources, but are they more of a danger than the five largest paper and lumber corporations?

Ask the residents of Santa Barbara who causes the worse beach litter—the tourists or the Union Oil Company? If you only watched television ads you'd get a completely distorted and inaccurate idea of what constitutes the worst attack on the biosphere.

In the political realm, the Council's campaigns and others directly initiated by the government support the war and attack the validity of independent protest activity, particularly by young people—see some of the Peace Corps ads which say in effect, "Stop yammering about the Dean and Do Something Constructive—Sign Up."

This bias goes so far that a conservative organization like Business Executives Move for Vietnam Peace has been turned down when it has asked for free public-service time.

It's even been refused when it's offered to buy time from a number of Washington area radio stations, including radio station WTOP, the CBS affiliate that is owned by the same company that owns the *Washington Post.* The station's position is that such issues are too complex and important to be discussed in this fashion; it says that all points of view are presented in its ordinary program format. The spot they wanted to put on the air was a statement by that notorious Bolshevik radical, the Honorable Marriner S. Eccles, former chairman of the Federal Reserve Board.

It read:

"The Vietnam War is responsible for the most serious financial problems in our country. But the real tragedy is not financial. It is the useless suffering of millions of people whose sons, husbands, and brothers are killed and maimed for life because of our incompetence and ill-advised leadership. We should be less interested in saving face and more interested in saving lives."

The announcer then comes on and tells you where to send for the Business Executives booklet, which may be another simple-minded comic book, but that's all right. Everyone has a right to advocate his case as he sees fit, even the owners of the Advertising Council—the wrong is in disguising Piggy Wiggy advocacy as public service while preventing others from having an equal chance at the front teat.

We laymen select a brand of aspirin because we see a funny ad for it on TV; we assume that our doctors choose the drugs they prescribe on weightier grounds.

But consider this ad appearing in a publication put out by doctors for doctors. On one side of the page there's an expensive four-color photograph of a nearly nude girl in a bikini. The chick is in a large, transparent, plastic bag held closed by a yellow satin ribbon. "Maybe she won't . . ." the copy reads as the string of periods draws our eyes to the next page where it says "but if she does get infective dermatitis . . . Fluonid-n cream is anti-infective, anti-pruritic and anti-inflammatory. It can break the infection-itch-scratch-inflammation cycle at any time." In the tiniest small print at the bottom of the page a physician with good eyes can read the warnings, precautions, and side effects.

This magazine, *Rx Sports and Travel,* "The Recreation and Leisure Magazine for Physicians," claims to be read by more doctors than any other publication. There are 204,707 subscribers, according to Business Publications Audit of Circulation. That is almost as many subscribers as the *Journal of the American Medical Association,* which the Standard Periodical Directory says has a circulation of 207,946.

Golf-club manufacturers, resort operators, and dude ranches respect the circulation of Rx enough to spend money advertising in it. Rx carries articles by Lee Trevino and pieces that begin, "A-weigh with the wind . . . Charter Yachting in the Caribbean. Avast there Aristotle and Jackie! Now almost anyone can 'own' a yacht for a tropical cruise."

All the drugs in Rx are for products manufactured by Marion Laboratories, Inc., of Kansas City, and the technique used on the doctors to get them to prescribe this stuff is exactly the same as that employed to sell Tide XK. "For the wet hot itch of athlete's foot," says another full page ad, " 'cool it' with Bluboro."

The height of something or other is reached in another reclame which shows (full page in color) a middle-aged woman on a beach. In the background is a man. The copy reads "Will his Angina come between them again tonight?" On the next page, the copy continues, "With the STABIL-IZER, Tender is the Night . . . Sexual excitement —particularly coitus—puts a physiological stress on many body systems including the heart. In the angina patient this 'overload' can mean seizure and pain . . . Today there is Nitro-Bid, the Stabil-izer. Prescribe Nitro-Bid for your angina pa-tients." Next to the text there is a picture of the same couple with expressions on their faces which, it must be supposed, indicate sexual satisfaction.

There is the three-page, four-color ad for Os-Cal/Mone. Another vivid photograph of a good looking, middle-aged woman. In big print it reads, "Perhaps when they are ready to give up 'The Pill' they should be taking another just to hold back time." The model in the photograph is explained by these words, "You've seen her be-fore, and the chances are you'll see her again: The Mrs. Robinson type, the smart, alert, zingy woman who looks and acts far younger than her menopausal years."

In case Rx should be dismissed as too atypical to be taken seriously, let's look at *Medical Eco-nomics,* which circulates to 193,000 doctors in private practice. It also is interested in the physi-cian at play. The issue dated September 29, 1969, has a piece not on yachts but on cruises, which tells the old family GP that "You must be careful to pick the right cruise. This is especially impor-tant now when more physicians are taking ex-tended vacations, cruises are becoming more popular with doctors, and members of medical societies often cruise en masse . . . A cruise, like a Cadillac, has become an American status symbol."

If the magazine reflects its readers' real inter-ests, you can understand why the profession has gotten the reputation for having a hemorrhaging money ulcer. It is obsessed with harvesting the long green. The pages are filled with stock tips, advice on mutual funds and tax shelters. "It's becoming steadily more difficult to find a good investment counselor to manage a small portfolio —one worth under $100,000," the magazine says commiseratingly to its readers. Nevertheless, *Medical Economics* tells its impoverished following not to give up but to invest in savings-and-loan company stock. Gains of 30 and 40 per cent are expected.

Should that not attract a down-on-his-luck orthopedic surgeon, he can do what a group of MD's in Bluffton, Indiana, did to make money. They formed a corporation to rent equipment to their local hospital. They didn't call it Hertz X-ray, but the profits are just fine. Seven per cent per annum with a share of stock which originally sold for $500 now worth $4,000. Ah, those lovely capital gains.

Regardless of how unusual the doctor's problem, if he writes in, the magazine has an answer for him: "I'm thinking of building new offices in a location that is otherwise attractive but next to a large cemetery . . . Does the cemetery's suggestive presence make this a poor choice of site?" Answer: "No . . . you can offset the site's minor disadvantage by landscaping it attractively and facing your entrance or waiting room away from the cemetery."

Another entertaining feature gives tips on how your doctor's office girl can collect bills more efficiently. It's illustrated with a picture of a chick in a nurse's uniform looking out from a frame in a dollar bill where George Washington usually poses. But even *Medical Economics* recognizes the old adage that pigs make money but hogs don't.

Another writer tells the doctors who mistake the ailing human body for a physiological Klondike, "You're not in any trouble financially. From the beginning of 1950 through June 30 this year, the general cost of living rose 55 per cent. Your fees, if you're typical, have risen 106.8 per cent during the same period. You can certainly afford to slow down . . . If the rate of increase in the first six months of 1969 should continue, the year will end with a total increase of some 9 per cent . . . An unusual rise in fees will almost certainly provoke fixed-fee schedules and a freeze. . . . The brutal fact is that many physicians aren't doing what they could and should do to avert such a catastrophe. They think only of making sure that, when the smoke clears, No. 1 will have been properly safeguarded."

The drug ads in *Medical Economics* are as entertaining as those in *Rx*: "Mr. Asthmatic worries a lot about air . . . help relieve his attacks—help keep him free of attacks with BRONKOTABS" —" 'For all the happiness mankind can gain/it is not a pleasure, but in rest from pain,' John Dryden—Give your patients rest from pain [with] Empirin Compound with Codeine"—"Loss of the ability of one generation to communicate with another is tragic. For a parent, the sense of guilt, shame and anguish following such a loss may lead to pathological depressions. When you diagnose depression, Tofranil may be indicated for relief."—"When you prescribe the pill should you recommend vaginal lavage?—Massengill liquid concentrate."

The best testimonial for medicine comes from the Jolly Green Giant who is shown in his family G.P.'s office listening while the doctor tells him, "You can go back to the Valley. But, no 'Ho. Ho. Ho's' for a week. And for sore throat pain, gargle with Chloraseptic."

Some people may think it both ironic and a betrayal that a President who's talked so much about getting the government out of this and that part of our lives should be the man who sent Congress a message on birth control. If there were ever an activity that we have considered nobody's damn business but our own it's how many kids we're going to have. No amount of keyhole-peeping by J. Edgar Hoover appears to be such an intrusion on our private liberties.

In effect, the message said the number of children we have is as much the state's business as our own. The message is correct, and the men who wrote it and the President who signed it should be given cigars and the same kind of hearty congratulations we accord to people who have so many babies. The only criticism you can make against it is that it didn't go far enough. However, it was probably as much as an elected politician could do in a country of many Catholics, sexual conservatives, and baby worshippers. Now it's for the rest of us to raise a supportive clatter.

The document predicts that within our lifetime there will be a hundred million more Americans. This country needs that only slightly less than an atom bomb attack. We're already running around like the old lady who had so many long-haired children she didn't know what to do. We can't accommodate the people we have without the most drastic changes in our living patterns.

When some people deprecate worries about our excessive production of babies, they say there will be enough food to go around. They talk about how we can avoid mass starvation by making protein comestibles out of fish scales or sea algae. They don't speculate on the pleasures of a life sustained in perpetual scarcity by processed kelp. For human beings there is a distinction between survival and living. They also overlook the fact that we are learning that many of the methods we use to increase food production —chemical fertilizers and insecticides, for instance—boomerang and turn out to be dangerous to health.

The easiest and most practical course is to cut back on our baby production. Nothing in the presidential message indicates the government's willingness to do that, even though its own figures demonstrate the need. The program envisioned by the administration draws a line at "infringing upon the religious convictions or personal wishes and freedom of any individual . . ."

That means the Catholic Church, the largest, best organized, and most moneyed enemy of birth control. There is some reason to believe that very large numbers of otherwise obedient Catholics use contraceptives, but you can't blame a politician for drawing back from asking such a hefty percentage of the voters to choose between themselves and their bishops. (Though one American bishop has resigned rather than buy the Vatican line.) The rest of us also are loathe to say much because it may smack of religious intolerance.

Yet something has to be said. The unchecked begetting of kids isn't like other religious practices. If an orthodox Jew wants to stay away from pork, that's his business. He isn't hurting anybody else, but that's not true of babies. What is true is that the seventy-year-old Italian celibates who cling to their aversion to contraceptives won't be alive to suffer the consequences of their erroneous teachings.

There's little we can do about the erroneous teachings, but do the taxpayers have to subsidize them? Do we have to give tax exemptions and financial aid to Catholic educational institutions while they teach children to follow practices that are going to ruin all of us? The least the government could do is support only private schools which teach and advocate birth control.

This is the barest of beginnings. The Catholic problem is the hierarchy's political opposition to population-reduction programs: Catholic birth rates aren't that different from everybody else's birth rates. We're all having too many children, but changing that isn't going to be easy. Many long-lived ideas must be stamped out first.

There is the notion, absurd in the era of the ABM, that many babies makes us militarily strong. This idea is not only connected with raising cannon fodder for the infantry but also with the masculine definition of virility. You're a man, you really got what it takes, lotsa you know what, because you can make a female pregnant. If you can do that you're a bull, a stud, a rooster. When we hear of a seventy-year-old male fathering a child, we make awed sounds and exclaim about what a man he must be. It's going to be hard to convince men that impregnating women is an anti-social act.

The case with women is more desperate. Many American women are brought up to believe their essential worthwhileness derives from motherhood and child-rearing. From the cradle they're schooled in attitudes that make them disdain any other occupation but the manufacturing of babies. Unmarried or childless women are spinsters, career girls, barren soil, somehow less than female.

Often people get married and have children because they have no other real choice. By their mid-twenties, women who're not married frequently are in a state of near panic as the source of likely husbands is used up, and they contemplate being single persons in a married people's world. It's somewhat better for a man, but not much. With both sexes the married majority tends to exclude the single minority during the years between twenty-five and fifty, when the men begin dropping dead. Everything is set up to encourage getting married and having unholy numbers of kids; the married couple with children gets tax incentives to reproduce, gets credit more easily, is considered a better risk for car insurance and is regarded as a potentially more stable and therefore more desirable employe.

People have children as a form of social security. A bunch of kids is a better health and retirement program than anything the government is offering or proposing. Moreover, we're weighed down with a lot of balderdash about perpetuating ourselves or that particular genetic pool known as our family through baby-making. Life ought to be sufficiently fulfilling and satisfying that we don't feel the urge to recoup our own disasters by living it out again through our children.

Limiting population production will exact other very large changes. We must divest ourselves of the belief that a stable or declining population is a sign of a stagnant or degenerate society. This means a good deal more than accepting abortion for any reason a woman wants it; it means reordering our economics. Our whole profit system is based on the proposition that the higher we can push the volume, the lower we can depress our per-unit costs. This once useful way of arranging things is outliving its utility. If some other way isn't found to provide Ford or GM with another basis for profit, we will perish from the most horrible and painful lung diseases.

Men like Ralph Nader have shown us that with cars, with drugs, with food and many other items what we need isn't more but better quality. But we've managed our economics and technology so that money is made out of quantity. Our big manufacturers have as much of a vested interest as the Pope in frustrating birth control.

Viewed from this point of view, our lunar escapades aren't high human adventures, man realizing his destiny, or the rest of the high-sounding bilge we've been dishing out; from this point of view it is tragic escapism, an enormous entertainment, a romance that distracts us from our peril unless one of our astronauts can find a new, large, inhabitable planet and get about three billion of us rocketed onto it while there is still time.

Love is still on Haight Street two years later, two years after the flower hysteria hit San Francisco, two years after the youth miracle that was going to redeem the world. Two years later Love is still here, the Persian woman with the outrageous red hair, big-bosomed lady serving her love-burgers from her sidewalk stand. Love is still here, still giving people free food, still broke, still looking after girls with babies and without husbands.

"The street's not changed, love," she said, wiping the counter and jingling the tiers of jewelry on her arms and around her neck. "Oh, some things are different, love. There's not so much acid. They take reds [seconal] a lot now, love. They're downers, but you can't sleep if you take enough of them. It makes them mean, but they're cheap—three for a dollar . . . Grass is $10 a lid [an ounce]."

LSD, which made the Haight, is believed in no more; the claims, therapeutic and theological, that used to be advanced for it are not now made. "Four or five years ago was the time to take LSD," said one of the nicer people who used to be in the Haight but doesn't go near the place now. "The world was sunny then, but you take acid now and then you stumble across some headline about a zillion people getting killed. Ugh! Yeck! The world has become more like New York than California. New York is death. New York is an old wino in the gutter twitching. You don't want to see that behind acid."

Despite Love, the street's changed. It's closed down, dying, a Virginia City, a skid row for young people, gray and horribly dangerous, a neighborhood of death. There have been more than twenty murders in the Haight this year alone, and some of them have been too awful. The photographs of the victims' bodies would make you vomit.

Nineteen-year-old Ann Jiminez, her hair shaved off her body, tortured all night to death by a group of nine boys and girls. "I literally hear shots every night," said John Hansen, a young man who saw seventeen-year-old Larry Watts shot down on the corner of Haight and Ashbury, the same corner that was used for the famous flower poster. "It was five o'clock in the afternoon and this guy with a high-powered rifle came out on the street from somewhere, aimed it, fired, killed the boy, and ran away." The latest murders took place week before last, two girls and a boy found shot through the head in an apartment.

A few of the people and the institutions that got so much publicity and attention during that brief time of national sentimentality about the Haight are still around. The famous free medical clinic is still operating, but only barely, just a few hours a day. Teddy Bear and Crazy Bob and

Mona and their organization called The Thirteenth Tribe are making much less of the scene, out of the dope business, apparently, staging rock concerts in the park and being denounced in the underground radical press as a bunch of shuckers.

The Krishna Consciousness Temple remains open with its blond, Hindu devotees from the Middle West, but most of the people who made the Haight whatever it was when it was at its Klondike height are gone. Beast, the prancing street madman who growled and made ferocious faces at the tourists, is gone; Iron Man, the one-armed dope dealer who kept his stash in his prosthesis, is gone; Peggy, the girl who opened the first hip-clothing store on the street, has fled to a downtown location.

For all that, Love may be right. It may not have changed. It was always violent, depressing, exploitative. The dope business is still the only subject anybody talks about. The speed houses where they shoot and sell methamphetamine are the same.

R is still dealing big. Only his initial may be used because the police would recognize his name. His pad is like always, somebody in the bedroom holding one end of a tourniquet in between clenched teeth so he can find a vein and shoot up, and somebody else in the kitchen arranging the fits (hypodermics) and measuring the white dope into nickel and dime ($5 and $10) packets.

"What's different now," R said, "is that speed's better than it used to be. There's not so much amphetamine poisoning, and you can ball on it, which you could never do before . . . Who do you have on Haight Street today? You have burn artists [dishonest dope peddlers], rip-offs [thieves], and snitchers [police finks]. It's them burning each other that's the cause of the killing. I got burned a couple of weeks ago. I went out on Haight Street and paid $10 for a lid of catnip."

As always in apartments like R's, there is a young girl or two, either trying to nest and make some kind of homey stability out of a crystal palace, or, like Venus, talking about leaving the Haight, leaving dope, going away; but she's been around a long time and it'll be hard for her to pick her way between delusion and illusion, reassemble the parts of her head and get out:

"The Haight's no place for an eighteen-year-old chick, man. It's no good for a chick like me. If I stay here I'm going to get busted. They'll bust this place and I'll lose custody of my children. I'll have a record and my husband will take them away . . . My mother has them.

"Gee, I shouldn't have come back to the Haight. I was living in this house in the country and it was beautiful, man, and nobody there had the same sign. My old man was a Sagittarius—you know how they are. He brought a different chick home every night. I'm a Cancer, so I couldn't stand it; and then I met Lon. Lon and I love each other. He wanted to come back to the Haight, so we came back here to R's, and he's dealing, too, but the place's going to get busted, man.

"I'm off speed. See, look at my arms. The veins are still discolored, but they're getting better. When I first started dope, people kept saying, 'Venus, don't do it, man.' But you can't tell people what to do. I just wish there had been somebody to keep me from doing it.

"The Haight's no place for an eighteen-year-old chick. I've really been so nervous and scared lately—the speed freaks in the house, you know. Lonnie was walking around with a submachine gun, trembling last night, and the street is not to be believed. I was with that cat who got shot in front of the Straight Theater. I mean, man, I don't like the police a lot, but what else can they do but what they do? I mean, when you're walking down the street and you can get shot and killed.''

Come to San Francisco; but bring your gun, lover.   ▬

> *Please allow me to introduce myself,*
> *I'm a man of wealth and taste.*
> *Pleased to meet you,*
> *Hope you guess my name.*
> *But what's puzzling you,*
> *Is the nature of my game.*
> *Just as any cop's a criminal,*
> *And all the sinners saints,*
> *. . . Just call me Lucifer, 'cause*
> *I'm in need of some restraints.*
> *—Fragments from "Sympathy for the Devil"*

As The Rolling Stones sang their hit song before some 300,000 people at the Altamont, California, Speedway the night of December 6, 1969, a young black man was chased from a point a few yards from where the famous English rock group was performing, beaten with weighted and sawed-off billiard cues, and stabbed to death. Only his white girl friend tried to save him.

The killers were bikers, members of the Hell's Angels, who were invited by some of the sponsors of The Rolling Stones' free concert to act as rentacops in exchange for $500 worth of beer. Another person died by drowning—a possible suicide—and two more were killed by a hit-and-run driver. From the reconstruction of what happened, it now appears that scores were beaten and injured, not only by bikers but also by others in the vast drunk and drugged crowd.

"Even the most incomplete medical reports show that this festival was dominated by violence. The volunteer medics treated more than just the usual bad trips and cut feet. They also treated dozens of lacerations and skull fractures. On top of these, they had an extraordinary number of bad trips—seemingly induced by the violence around them. People sitting near the stage said they could feel the wave of paranoia spreading through the stoned crowd with each beating. Acid plus muggings equaled terror and revulsion," wrote *Rolling Stone* magazine, no relation to the musical group.

Although the *Village Voice* reported some of what happened, it remained for the magazine, the best rock and youth culture publication in the country, to make a full picture of this horrible and bloody day. By using eleven reporters and thousands of words, *Rolling Stone* (circulation 100,000) did the journalistic job that might have been done by the other media which worked so hard to describe what Woodstock was about.

It was *Rolling Stone* magazine that found a close-up eyewitness to the murder:

"I didn't know his name or anything, but he was standing alongside of me. You know, we were both watching Mick Jagger [the Stones' lead singer], and a Hell's Angel, the fat one . . . reached over and grabbed the guy beside me by the ear and hair, and yanked on it, thinking it was funny, you know, kind of laughing.

"This guy shook loose, and the Hell's Angel hit him in the mouth and he fell back into the crowd . . . He tried to scramble through the crowd to run from the Hell's Angel, and four other Hell's Angels jumped on him . . . He didn't give any verbal provocation or anything. So they're chasing him through the crowd. They're hitting him and one Hell's Angel pulled out a knife and stabbed him in the back . . . He (the victim) pulled out a gun and held it up in the air, you know . . . like that was kind of his last resort . . . He was too scared to shoot . . . And one of the Hell's Angels grabbed the gun . . . and then stabbed him in the back . . . He came running kind of toward me and then he fell down on his knees, and then the Hell's Angel . . . started kicking him in the face about five times . . .

"Then one of them kicked him on the side and he muttered some words. He said, 'I wasn't going to shoot you.' That was the last words he muttered."

Rolling Stone magazine is owned, edited, and written by younger people in their twenties. Yet they went to the trouble and thought it necessary to put out a full account of the Altamont Free Festival when the larger media, controlled by older people, continued to crank out Woodstock goosh in their big end-of-the-decade wrapups.

We're going through a second flower-child cycle. Two and a half years ago, when the roses and delphiniums hit, the older response was to treat the flower petals as proof that a love/peace/gift-giving ethic had suddenly taken hold of the children whose parents have made Vietnam, ICBM, and MIRV. It's tempting to gulp up salt water drops in the corner of the eye and exclaim, "Lo! Behold! Our children are saints and shame us. They cling together in huge numbers to make peace and music, and neither do they offer violence, one to another, nor rob and cheat."

This is parental escapism, and it's as powerful as the dope their children smoke. By now we should all be old enough to know that peace and virtue are realizable only through foresight, planning, practice, and work. The difference between Woodstock and an Altamont is that the one had them and the other didn't.

The people who put Woodstock together worked at the preparations for weeks beforehand. They didn't hire a bunch of racist hoods to play cop, but got real policemen who knew the best way to preserve the public peace is to build as much of a social structure as possible so that order would be preserved, as it usually is, by the voluntary cooperation of the people in the community. As a fallback, there were policemen, individuals of good judgment who use the law, not sweet emotions, as a baseline for deciding what to do.

Altamont was put together in three or four days. Two reasons are given for its happening. One is that The Rolling Stones—the group, not the publication—had charged such outrageous prices during their American tour they had to throw a freebie if they ever wanted to come back; the other explanation is they wanted to make a movie, a rush job that would cash in on the festival frenzy before the Woodstock movie came out.

"It may surprise many of the people who suffered Altamont," *Rolling Stone* said in its January 21, 1970, issue, "to discover that they were, in effect, unpaid extras in a full-production, color motion picture."

The rock group got their movie, photographed by Albert and David Maysles, makers of *The Salesman*. People who've seen the Altamont footage say that it clearly shows the murder, and so the young imitate the old and learn from them.

If Altamont was greed, cruelty, irresponsibility in the true meaning of that word; if it was exploitation of people and the land, which was left littered, then you know where the young people found their models.

They have other models, too, for it should also be reported that some people did try to stop the violence and the bullying. One member of The Jefferson Airplane tried to save somebody from a beating and was cold-conked unconscious for his trouble, but a sane social order doesn't allow justice and decency to depend upon individual acts of heroism.

Most people aren't heroes. They react as this attendee who wrote of himself in the San Francisco weekly *Good Times* as follows, "I don't like authority ever, so I didn't like the Angels much either. But how to relate to them? How to help? I'm not a fighter. And talking was out. Hence, I was as helpless as anyone. Impotent. That's the word."

The problem was compounded by the massive use of dope, all kinds of dope, alcohol, acid, mescaline, reds, speed, you name it. The constant anti-grass harassment has pushed the use of really bad crap. Dope, and that must include alcohol which is getting very big among the young again, makes people defenseless, particularly vulnerable in large crowds. They don't know how to maintain.

"I kept thinking we are so stupid," writes Sandy Darlington, the attendee quoted above, "so unable to cope with anything practical. Push forward, yes, smoke dope, yes. But maintain? Never. We don't know how. We've been coddled, treadmilled, straight-teethed, and vitamin-pilled, but we don't know what to do."

There will be many more festivals where all of these problems will have to be worked through. Any attempts to suppress festivals will be foolish and wrong; but pressure must be applied to see that they're well planned and commercially successful, yes, but not humanly exploitative. This means that we can't act like Governor Claude Kirk of Florida, who put a young man in jail at a festival because he sassed his excellency; nor can it mean that we smile buttercups and say, "Run off, young dears, get stoned and make love, you tender, saintly things." ■

Senator John O. Pastore (D-R.I.) adjusted his toga awhile back and declared, "We're going to spend a lot of money to remove crime from the streets. I think we ought to spend some to remove pollution from the minds of our people." With that it was announced we are going to have the Surgeon General spend a million dollars to study the causal relations, if any, between television and violence.

The study is supposed to be finished in a year, but don't count on learning much from it, because the social sciences do not now have the ability to render more than informed and highly fallible opinion. NBC is also spending half a million dollars on what you might call a counterstudy, which will doubtless show the Old Roman from Rhode Island is wrong to think TV is helping "to break down the morals of our nation."

If you don't want to think about violence in our country seriously, blame television for causing it. You can treat it as an electronic outside agitator—an out-of-town troublemaker in a cathode tube. In the course of the last five hundred years, this has been done with the legitimate theater, radio, movies, and movable type. It's a good ploy, a good way to whip up a mob of unthinking people who'll be too excited to consider the proposition that some of the causes of violence might be found in the United States Senate.

The indisputably most violent hour on American television begins at 6:30 when Walter Cronkite and Huntley-Brinkley metamorphose out of the air waves to show us what our armies and fleets are doing today. It's Senator Pastore and his colleagues who've voted the money to fight the perpetual, defensive war on the other side of the globe, so if the networks are guilty of incitement it's hard to see why they are more guilty than the man from Rhode Island, who accuses them of "recklessness" and "dereliction."

You'll never be able to prove it, but it seems that the color footage of General Loan, the South Vietnamese police chief, murdering an unarmed, helpless captive did have some effect on many American youths and some older people, too. It could not have been more graphic. You could see the white of the man's brains spurting out of his smashed skull.

Millions did see it and they got some experience of war from it. Other millions saw Metromedia's presentation of "Face of War," the documentary on the Marine company in which it seemed that you were watching most of the cast being killed or maimed.

It's very good for us as a people to see these terrible, unspeakable things happening to our soldiers and to the people of other countries. Except for a portion of our fighting men, we haven't had the firsthand experience with war that so many other people have had in this, the most murderous, the most inhumane sixty-nine years of recorded history. As the inhabitants of the most militarily powerful nation on the globe, we should know what we do with our force.

What effect does it have on us, citizens of a proud, bellicose, mighty nation, to watch death night after night in our living rooms? Maybe these awful spectacles are simply gladiatorial games in a vacuum tube to which we've become indifferent like the citizens of Rome.

After seeing the nightly news, it's hard to believe that most people would care to do anything more violent than throw up or cry out. It seems strained to suggest that after such film footage the ordinary little TV stage dramas would be taken for more than what they are, mildly diverting action stories. After looking at the real thing, who's going to be bothered by Matt Dillon

or the Name of the Game, with their little artificial killings?

Outside of the news, the only really serious
violence on television occurs Saturday morning
when those cartoon characters bash each other
silly. This, of course, is socially useful violence
because it gets the little ones accustomed to the
angry, striving, competitive life that our most
influential ideologues tell us separates us from
Communists, Swedes, Indians, or anybody else
who doesn't accept the social Darwinism, the
survival-of-the-fittest principle that we call the
ratrace while we're drinking our after-work mar-
tinis.

The truly violent medium is the movies. In its
goriest moments TV's never come close to the
murder scene in *Bullitt,* a celluloid passage that
would make Quakers out of half the Pentagon. In
some of the better movies, like Jean-Luc God-
ard's *Weekend,* violence serves as a tool for describing not only the institutions that the Rhode
Island Senator serves but our civilization.

In this movie the countryside is cluttered with
car wrecks, a flaming automobile junk yard.
There are bodies everywhere, but they look more
like the store mannequins that you've seen
dragged out onto the streets in newsreel footage
of race riots, the bodies of people turned into
neurasthenic plaster by the violence of a civilization that kills itself off cursing in traffic jams.

Juxtaposed against such a moral analysis of
the causes of violence, Senator Pastore's hector-
ing of the TV networks not only begins to look
frivolous and eccentric but also like a positive
attempt to distract us from seriously considering
a problem that has become our collective, national obsession. Increasingly we resemble the
homicidal maniac who used the lipstick of his
victims to write the police messages imploring
them to "Stop me, please, before I do this again."

here are two Californias. There is the California of the beaches, the mountains, the good places to eat, the resorts, the places where you do your California dreamin'. The other California is of the valleys, flat, hot, laborious, where they grow the food, the fruit, the grapes.

Bakersfield, Delano in the San Joaquin are in the second California of stoop-labor and heat. So is Brawley, a green place in the desert of the Imperial Valley, about thirty miles from the Mexican border. It's not too much of a place with its drive-ins and its used-car lots, their plastic pennants forever fluttering. It's a town that reminds you a little bit of Greenwood, Mississippi, except that the government-subsidized irrigation has made it richer and there are palm trees, those giraffes of the vegetable world.

The other day there was a Mexican man on the highway which runs south from Coachella through desert where there is nothing to see but sand, scrubble brush, and the signs of real estate developers proclaiming the coming of lakes, marinas, and planned retirement cities. A robust old man he was, not feeble, but bowlegged, redfaced, wearing a straw hat and carrying a sign which read, "Slow Down, Marchers Ahead." Heavy, articulated diesel semis hauling onions and alfalfa and sugar beets drove with undiminished speed and noise past him. Their wind almost blew him off the hot highway, but he held his position, following them with his head and his eyes as they rolled off into the desert. He wouldn't give up.

A half-mile up the road came the marchers. They wouldn't give up either. There weren't many of them, maybe forty or fifty grape strikers walking down the highway being led by a woman in a straw cowboy hat. She carried the gold and white canvas painting of Our Lady of Guadalupe on a staff. Slightly behind her on either side were men carrying the American and Mexican flags.

For four years the Mexican-Americans have had their strike, their *huelga* as they call it, against the grape growers and for social justice. They and their leader, Cesar Chavez, have marched, picketed, vigiled, struck, fasted, implored, and prayed to little purpose. Only eleven companies have signed contracts with the union. But they're like the old man. They don't give up. Instead they think up more tricks and stunts to perform so they can catch the national attention and press their claims on somebody who will honor them.

This latest contretemps which ended on the Mexican border is an attempt to hook up with the Mexican labor movement to prevent the importation of strikebreakers from the other side, something the American government is supposed to stop but does not. It is another example of the growing number of complaints that the government primarily serves the powerful and the well organized and not the weak and disorganized.

Recently Washington has paid the farmworker's union some attention. However, Chavez wishes the Secretary of Labor hadn't bothered because he regards the administration's proposals for new legislation as a union-busting scheme wrapped up in the language of philanthropy. "For thirty-five years the growers have opposed all legislation, they've been against everything, including child-labor regulation and minimum wages, but now they turn around and support this law," says Chavez, a quiet, pious man around whom a cult of admiration akin to Martin Luther King's is building.

Chavez, like King, has integrated nonviolence into his working philosophy of life, but unlike

King, Chavez can be very specific about law and technicality. He is not only a leader of "la raza," as the Mexican-Americans collectively call themselves, but a man who heads a labor union and wants the protection of government-supervised union elections, something farmworkers have never had. He doesn't want what the Nixon administration is offering because he believes it would put farm workers under the jurisdiction of the grower-controlled Department of Agriculture, would forbid strikes during harvest time, and then, after defanging and disarming the union, would force it into compulsory arbitration. It would also make secondary boycotts of grapes in supermarkets illegal. It's been the attempt to boycott grapes being sold by supermarket chains that have dramatized the strike and spread the word of it across the country. The marchers here carried signs saying "Abajo Safeway" (Down with Safeway).

"They should give us a Wagner Act as they did the other unions in the 1930's when they were young and weak. They should give us the same protection and freedom the Wagner Act gave the other unions for an equal length of time. If we had an equal chance in the local courts and in the importation of strikebreakers, we could beat them in the fields anytime," says Chavez, who emphasizes it was only after the unions were organized under the Wagner Act that restrictions on boycotts and striking were put on them in the form of the Taft-Hartley law, which was designed to limit the power of overly strong unions but which effectively destroys new unions.

When the marchers reached Brawley they were joined by several hundred high school kids who're in revolt because the school has forbidden them to wear a button proclaiming the "Mexican-American Revolution," or so says Loupe Sabala, their eighteen-year-old leader. "They said our button meant violence even after we explained that we meant revolution through education. They said they were for our goals but the button would cause so much turmoil that they had to ban it," he explains.

The students' complaints are the usual ones you can hear from minority kids if you care to listen to them talk about their schools. They say they are discouraged by the teachers from trying to enroll in the academic classes that lead to college and the professions, that they are put down, that their culture and history is ignored, and that kids who speak Spanish only are dumped into classes for the mentally retarded. Now they are aroused, imbued with a new sense of *la raza* that makes them identify themselves with all Mexican-American aspirations and pushes them to take their place in the line of march when their parents hang back with the frightened conservatism of older people whose whole lives have been one long squelch.

They are marching in the valleys of the second California. The laws of Washington or not, they will walk on, hopefully without violence, hopefully still believing in our system of government and economics, hopefully still reciting their litany of militance and progress:

> *Que Viva La Huelga!*
> *Que Viva La Virgen de Guadalupe!*
> *Que Viva César Chavez!*
> *Que Viva La Causa!*
> *Que Viva La Raza!*   ■■■

It was CBS that showed the nurse bending over the crib, hypodermic in hand, to give the tiny, three-week-old junkie a fix. The junkie is the child of a Harlem mother who is also a junkie; the infant was born with a monkey on his back. This little baby will have to go through the trauma of being weaned from heroin before he is weaned from milk, and CBS reports that there are lots of children in ghetto hospitals similarly blessed.

This story was told by CBS, but it might have been NBC or ABC or the *New York Times* or *Life,* any of the big, rich mass media who have ethics which urge them, for God's sake, to go out there and show people how hideously varied is this pluralistic society we sometimes boast of.

They perform a service, running their sight-seeing buses to the scenic disasters of American society. There is a tour-like quality to these excursions in which we're shown miserable, sick, dazed people in their hovels because they're presented to us in much the same way happier tours show other travelers the Grand Tetons or the Big Sur or the Delaware Water Gap. "There it is," our journalistic tour guide seems to be saying to us, "so pitiful, so painful that it could only be the work of God. Unhappiness on such a scale couldn't be fabricated by man."

This frightful portrayal of the screaming maimed in ghetto and plantation, in barrio, Appalachian vale, and Indian reservation is customarily presented to us as a phenomenological event, a result without a cause. Like a mountain or an earthquake, it just is, and after reporting it we're invited to go on to the next segment of the television program or the next article in the magazine, which may be Jean Claude Killy or

Janis Joplin or that one member of the Ford family who doesn't have the smarts to keep his consumption moderately inconspicuous while he plays the game of responsible businessman.

From time to time some commentators try to ascribe causality to these scenes. The preferred explanation is pathological. Society is envisioned as a three-thousand-mile-long human body that's got sick spots on it here and there—like "slum cancer." After some especially heinous exposé, the more exuberant may go so far as to write of a "sick society."

No more illuminating but medically more impressive is Joe Alsop's "locomotor ataxia." The famous columnist recently wrote this paragraph: "These hideous diseases of the school system are so serious that they can imaginably cause the actual breakdown of public education in New York, yet they are precisely like locomotor ataxia. In other words, they are really by-products of the still more terrible ghetto-disease," which our social diagnostician tells us has now entered "the dreaded tertiary phase."

The mass media doesn't use this method of understanding when it looks at the domestic problems of our major ideological opponent. Wheat shortages in Russia are both explained and blamed on their system of government and economics. The same systematic analysis is applied to faulty Russian automobiles, their housing shortage, and their technology—or at least it was until they shot up Sputnik.

The closest we seem to come to understanding why what's wrong is wrong is by citing history. We explain ghettos and Indian reservations by pointing to the past. This has two advantages: the first is that all the villains are dead, and the second is that there's nothing you can do about history; the very explanation also serves as an excuse for not doing anything about the present.

But if history can be used to make a plausible

if not a convincing case to show why black people are exploited today, it's not even plausible for telling us why we have some of the same problems the Russians have. Why does New York City have a horrendous housing shortage and why has it had it for nearly thirty years? Why do so many people make the same complaints about our new buildings that they make about the new buildings in Russia, namely that they are cheaply put together and don't work half the time? Why is General Motors always calling back zillions of cars which the manufacturers suspect weren't built right or weren't designed properly?

These are questions that we have enormous difficulty answering or even asking. Our systemic analysis of Russian society makes us see why their cars don't run right and a proportion of their people are hungry. Our lack of systemic analysis of American society has blinded us to hunger here and made us oblivious to the defects in our own social and economic processes.

One of the reasons we haven't looked at our society as a number of interlocking systems is that few tools to do it have been available. You can't analyze a social system if you accept all of its deep-down, unspoken assumptions. You have to get outside of it, unless you're content to be a tepid reformer, a person who patches, fixes, and fusses over details.

To see ourselves we need alien viewpoints; we need foreign eyes to pick over and diagnose our faults on a systemic basis. That was a function the old left might have performed, but twenty years ago the Communists and Socialists were so completely stamped out you can hardly find one in an American university or on an American newspaper. Even now the girls at the office going-away party sign the gift card, "From your fellow employees," never "From your fellow workers," because that expression hints at a different way of looking at things.

It's too late to bring the old-time Communists and Socialists back. Nobody believes in them. They haven't done well enough where they've tried to build socialism. To the concerned and idealistic of today, Russia appears to be worse than the light that failed, it seems like a left-handed America, more fumbling, more brutal, and less able to cope than we.

Both American left and right are laboring to build suitable systems of analysis, but it's hard to do, coming out of thirty years of high-pressure national consensus, when Jerry Rubin and Barry Goldwater are disregarded as irresponsible, extremist nuts. Yet the Rubins and the Goldwaters do look at America differently, and without them we're going to ride forever in a CBS tour bus. ▰

> *Between the idea*
> *And the reality*
> *Between the motion*
> *And the act*
> *Falls the shadow.*
> —T. S. Eliot, "The Hollow Men."

Six months ago the President sent a message to Congress suggesting it do something for population control. Nothing has happened except more babies have been conceived while demographers shuddered, ecologists shook their heads, and scientists advanced their inquiries as to how and when the human race will expire.

There is doubt about how exactly we will do away with ourselves, although very little hesitation to predict we will. The optimists forecast universal, atomic euthanasia, but the newer and now-dominant opinion looks for the end to come miserably in the ingeniously horrible forms of science fiction. Not with a bang but a whimper.

In this lugubrious debate there is a school of thought that foresees our going the way of a country like Afghanistan, where the earth itself suffers from incurable maladies, according to Robert and Leona Rienow in the book *Moment in the Sun* (Sierra Club–Ballantine, 1969, 95 cents): "Not only are the surface waters laden with diseases and plagues, but the lack of proper sewage disposal over the centuries has caused permeation by the pollution of the sparse soils until the deep aquifer—that vast and mystical lake of fresh water underlying Earth's surface—has become universally contaminated . . . to live in a country where the very soil in our garden and the ground water under our feet . . . are writhing with cholera, hepatitis, tuberculosis, typhus, dysentery, typhoid, diphtheria, polio, viruses, and hundreds of other plagues—where to drill a well in one's backyard is to challenge death— must indeed be the ultimate horror."

A different line of inquiry speculates that we're polluting ourselves into another ice age. MIT's *Technology Review* (October/November 1969) says, ". . . there is increasing evidence that urban and industrial pollution, perhaps aided by agricultural pollution, is in large part responsible for decreasing the surface temperature . . ." This is not yet an established fact; indeed there are few established facts; the scientists who study these things tell us the workings of the global systems we are upsetting aren't understood.

What they do agree on is that if we continue as we are, when all the facts are established it will be too late to alter them and we will die. It is also established that much of what we needlessly do has awesome repercussions in nature. The same issue of the same magazine blames the pumping of fluid wastes into the earth for three earthquakes in Denver, Colorado, in 1967, while the same year a dam in India is thought to have caused a quake that killed more than two hundred people.

Every publication that devotes itself to the subject repeatedly warns that these terrible consequences aren't local but affect the planet. It's not just the air over New York or Los Angeles that brings particulate death, but the air, period; all the air in Maine, in the Bahamas, the North Woods, the atmosphere of the planet. And what's our response? About $100,000 a year is being spent by the government to study what we're doing to our air.

It's natural to defer spending money to fend off future ills if you know they're far enough in the future. We don't. We know the contrary. Change is changing faster than change ever changed before. Only people as old as the Speaker of the House of Representatives can safely bet that they'll die before the deluge or the plague or the asphyxia or the consummate quake gobbles us up. The present generation of congressional committee chairmen may be the last old people to die quiet, natural, dignified deaths.

In their complacency at having been smart enough to get themselves born before 1900, they're indifferent to the rest of us who're stranded and catching at mouthfuls of air in the twentieth century. For six months they've not only ignored the President's modestly inadequate birth-control proposals, they've passed a tax bill which encourages baby production.

Instead of increasing the exemption for children, what they should have done is pass a bill providing no exemption for any child born to a middle-income family ten months after the bill was signed; upper-income families should have a stiff, rising scale of negative exemptions. Under such a system people making, say, $20,000 a year, would have an extra $1,000 of taxable income to pay on if they have one child, $2,500 for two, and so on.

The reason isn't to make parents, rather than childless people, pay for schools, but because a rich child is a much greater ecological burden than a poor one. On the average, one American in his lifetime will use 21,000 gallons of leaded gasoline, 56 million gallons of water, 10,150 pounds of meat, and 28,000 pounds of milk. That's an average, so you can guess what the consumption of the rich and even the not so rich is. Twenty-nine per cent of all families now own two cars.

We can't go on like this. There are 70 million cars on the road now, four million more than there were last year. Either we give up our cars, our jets, our nice homes, our buying and using or we limit the number of Americans allowed to come into existence. Even so we may have to do both. It already costs $50 a year to empty each garbage can in New York City, and there's no place to put the garbage after we've collected it. What are we going to do when the millions of young people now reaching family formation age strike out on their own, with their own cars, their own garbage production, their own demand for housing?

The population bomb has already been detonated. We've had Hiroshima, are we also going to get Nagasaki? If the children are afflicted with the same rabid rabbitism that took hold of their Eisenhower-era mating parents, human babies are going to become as valuable as mongrel puppies.

There's nothing new about this information or the conclusions drawn here. The only reason the

words have to be said again and many times over
is that the people who run things are too lethargic
even to protect their own comfort or theirs or
their children's future. Every kind of opportunity
is missed. Congress passes changes in the Social
Security Act but fails to provide large pensions
for childless couples marrying after the law takes
effect. They do that in spite of everybody telling
them that one of the reasons people have children is for social security.

The states and the courts crawl in the direction
of legalizing abortions like pregnant turtles dropping fertilized eggs as they belly across the sand.
Finally we'll have legalized abortions, but how's
that going to save us if our population is up over
the 300 million mark?

The media which can bang pots and ring bells
for the most insignificant causes have yet to put
on the first anti-baby campaign. Where are the TV
spots giving people a realistic assessment of
what kind of a life that baby's going to live?
Where are the billboards proclaiming fast-breed-
ing animals are pests? Why are we still making
over multi-children mothers and having Father
of the Year contests?

The businessmen and economists are also
going to have to find another way. Their stock
solution to all problems is increasing the Gross
National Product. A balanced budget, public
works, higher profits, everything good is supposed to come from stepping up the volume of
production—enlarging the parameters, as economists like to say. We don't even have a theo-
retical model of a balanced economy that isn't
expanding but is accomplishing its tasks by re-
maining stable. Laissez-faireists, Keynesians,
Marxists, all of them rely on infinite growth of
production, but this can't be. Fifty million more
fast babies aren't 50 million more customers—
they're a disaster. The system must be adjusted

so that a way can be found to make money while holding production constant or even, God forbid, cutting back.

"This is the way the world ends," wrote the poet, "Not with a bang but a whimper." Or a gasp, or a clutch or a groan or a cough or a frail exhalation. Exactly how eludes our knowing. The last moment may come before the planet can no longer sustain human life; it may come when the press of too many crazy people killing and cutting each other destroys our human communities. That's what some social scientists believe. If we allow it to happen we *are* the hollow men of the poem, the stuffed men, leaning together, head-pieces filled with straw, and the last sound *shall* be rats' feet over broken glass.　■

'Cause you know I'm here
Everybody knows I'm here
Yeah, I'm a hoochie-coochie man
Everybody knows I'm here.

The recollections are imprecise, but it appears to have been toward the end of World War II that the hoochie-coochie man himself came into the bar that Leonard and Phil Chess owned at 47th and Cottage Grove in Chicago. Leonard is dead; the hoochie-coochie man is laid up in traction after a car accident; so the only one around is Phil, and he says, "That's where it started, the blues."

The hoochie-coochie man was born McKinley Morganfield, but he's known to a wider public as Muddy Waters, the man who, as much as any other, took the blues of the rural South, and in

the late forties and fifties, made them urban. He
was not the only one, of course. There are
younger and older ones who are dead and
legendary. Like Sonny Boy Williams:

> *Now me and my baby we talked last night*
> *And we talked for nearly an hour*
> *She wanted me to go down to the Welfare*
> *Store*
> *And get a sack of that Welfare flour.*

They depicted the translation of millions of
people from country to city. In music and verse
their work represents the fullest statement of
this explosive social event, of what the city, the
welfare, the white North has meant to lower-
class black men. Their work demonstrates that
the pain and indignity of the ghetto isn't something that more self-conscious, more political
black artists invented. In the next stanza, Sonny
Boy sings,

> *I say, I'll do anything in the world for you*
> *I don't want to go down to that Welfare*
> *Store.*

In the middle forties, blues were nowhere. It
was disreputable music even among hip urban
blacks who had ears only for jazz. "You'd see a
little girl go into a record shop," Phil Chess recalls. "She'd wait till every one was gone—all
the other customers—an' she'd go up to the man
and ask for her blues record in a whisper and
have him put it in a bag so nobody could see. The
youngsters felt the blues were poking fun at the
race."

They couldn't stay away from it, however. It
spoke to them because it's very strong music. It
makes no concessions. That it now enjoys some
popularity is probably due to the ten years of
preparation provided by rock and roll and
rhythm and blues which have opened people up
and trained them to listen to the original, real

thing. Even so, a lot of people may find the words too strong and the music too assonant.

That is why Chess Records, the company Leonard and Phil eventually founded, is advertising its new series of blues albums as "the hard stuff" with a picture of Sonny Boy and Muddy and Little Walter and Howlin' Wolf and the others as labels on whiskey bottles. Six of the series, which will ultimately run to more than thirty albums, have been released. They contain many songs and performances that are so obscure only blues maniacs and musicologists have ever had a chance to hear them. They also contain a large number of cuts that have never been released as well as many that will be immediately familiar to students of the culture of American cities.

They might never have been recorded if the Chess brothers hadn't owned that bar. They met Muddy there, and it was he who touted them on to other blues men who they put on records. But the bar was more than an occasion for their encounter with the blues; the bar taught them about the murderous, insecure, and fractional life out of which the blues arrived. Phil Chess remembers fights; he remembers having a man put a gun at his head; he remembers Pistol Pete, the South Side cop walking down 47th Street smacking people across the face, Pistol Pete who, says the urban folk myth, killed thirteen men and maybe more.

> *I'm going over to 3rd Alley*
> *Lord, but I'm gonna carry my 45*
> *Because, you know, ain't many men*
> *Goes there and comes back alive.*

(These verse quotations are all from *The Blues Line,* compiled by Eric Sackheim, Grossman Publishers, Inc. 1969, an exceptionally fine book, but priced out of reach at $20.)

That's the way Walter Rowland sings it in his

"45 Pistol Blues." That's the way the Chess brothers, immigrant Polish boys to the Chicago Jewish slum, learned to live and appreciate the blues. They were scrambling and fighting, too. Their bar—they had a string of them before they got into records full time—was an after-hours joint run twenty-four hours a day. It was a business experience that prepared them to understand the blues which they treated in a tough and rasping way, never divorcing it from scrounging a buck, never killing it off by putting it under glass in the Library of Congress.

Phil says they got into the recording business because they saw a market which wasn't being catered to, but it was the sag end of the record business. They peddled their first releases to ghetto record stores out of the back seat of their car. It must have been a disordered, catch-as-catch-can business. Some of the cuts being released now in this new Vintage series were never even entered onto the master book; they were discovered by Tom and Cathy Swan, whom the company has hired to produce these albums.

They found one tape of Leonard Chess and Sonny Williamson trying to record a song called "Little Village." The two men grouse and cuss and make tired sounds at each other in a rare example of the fusion of art, commerce, and daily life. "What really got us into it was being in business with colored people. We got the feel of it," says Phil Chess, but it wasn't a formal, studied feel. "I couldn't read you a musical score if you showed me one. I never knew what paying for an arrangement was until 1955 or '56." The Swans have searched everywhere for the proper photographs to put on the album covers.

They have a great one of Little Walter, scarred, squinting, smiling, and crazy. Tom Swan who knew this man that many people think was the finest harp who ever did the blues, says he drank way too much whiskey. Then he got beaten up by a cop and "his brains got leaky." He died (February 15, 1968) before he was forty, thus proving out that the blues are still precarious and disreputable.

Magic Sam died in a car accident a few weeks ago. Many others are dead or have disappeared, and of the blues men that keep at it, few make money. Their greatest following is among white college students, but even so they get played only on obscure FM stations, and many record stores are skeptical about stocking their records. Imitation white blues bands are more popular and make more money, but not better music.

"The black person can freak out in his own way, but he knows the Man is around," says Tom Swan, "so with the black blues musician, he has a controlled reaction. It's like a disciplined violence." The white blues people are seldom able to master this restraint of premeditated art. They tend to be like Joplin, too loose, too wild, too rough, but their music is popular, in part, perhaps, because many of us white people need to project our Bacchanalian yearnings onto others in safe ways.

Too bad. Father Blues is the recurring source of most of our native music. Hard stuff, and when we do this we make it next to impossible to enjoy Father Blues' art. We also destroy the message which is more and different than white release and happy, heathenistic white pain.

> *I'm so glad*
> *Good whiskey have made it through*
> *Well well, I'm so glad*
> *Good whiskey have made it through*
> *Well now, it have saved my wife from dying*
> *Ooo well well, and saved my sweetheart*
> *   too.*

The paperback edition of *The Autobiography of Malcolm* X is now in its eighteenth printing. More than one million copies have been sold. It is used in so many classrooms that Grove Press puts out a special discussion guide for it. Among high school and college students it is endlessly read, passed on, and talked about. Che may not live, but Malcolm does.

He deserves to. Like Augustine and the other great confessional writers, Malcolm is able to fuse ideas—theology, politics, psychology—into his own personal experience and tell it so you live it with him. A lot of people before him, some of them very good writers, had written about how the black man, robbed of his identity by the white man, would scar and deface himself in order to ape his oppressor, but probably nothing in our literature matches Malcolm's description of his first conk or process of hair straightening. His friend Shorty did the job on him in Shorty's slum room in Boston's Roxbury ghetto.

"I took the little list of ingredients Shorty had printed out for me and went to a grocery store, where I got a can of Red Devil lye, two eggs, and two medium-sized white potatoes. Then at a drugstore near the poolroom I asked for a large jar of vaseline, a large bar of soap, a largetoothed comb and a fine-toothed comb, one of those rubber hoses with a metal spray-head, a rubber apron, and a pair of gloves. 'Going to lay on that first conk?' the drugstore man asked me," writes Malcolm, who narrates how Shorty mixed this mess up and put it on his kinky, red hair. "I gritted my teeth and tried to pull the sides of the kitchen table together. The comb felt as if it was raking my skin off. My eyes watered, my nose was running. I couldn't stand it any longer;

I bolted to the washbasin. I was cursing Shorty with every name I could think of," but then he tells the rest:

"My first view in the mirror blotted out the hurting. I'd seen some pretty conks, but when it's the first time, on your own head, the transformation, after the lifetime of kinks, is staggering . . . on top of my head was this thick, smooth sheen of shining red hair—real red—as straight as any white man's. How ridiculous I was!"

Scholars can write their way through libraries talking about the black man's identity problem and never come as close to explaining it as Malcolm does in that portion of his book. This may be the reason for its enduring popularity with white kids who do so much want to understand and share the pain.

Malcolm was more than a passive figure, studying himself and noting it down. Malcolm was the action principle, or, as he says, "My gun was ready if I heard a mosquito cough." He was a crazy adolescent who did things and was involved in things that young people are deep into now. Like the draft. Malcolm ate at Alice's Restaurant before Arlo Guthrie was born. Read part of his description of his interview with the Army induction shrink during World War II:

"I knew I was going to send him back to the books to figure out what kind of a case I was. Suddenly, I sprang up and peeped under both doors . . . and then I bent and whispered fast in his ear. 'Daddy-o, now you and me, we're from up North here, so don't you tell nobody . . . I want to get sent down South. Organize them nigger soldiers, you dig? Steal us some guns, and kill up crackers.' That psychiatrist's blue pencil dropped, and his professional manner fell off in all directions."

Malcolm knew the souls of white folks. A World War II white shrink either had to declare him nuts or have him jailed. Malcolm knew that because he knew every American white man fears black retribution; Malcolm knew it all about the blue-eyed devils and expressed it best. The Stokely Carmichaels, the Rap Browns, even the most eloquent successors like Eldridge Cleaver have only been able to embellish but not substantially improve on Malcolm X's understanding of the tormentor.

He had the servile experience and that may be the reason he understood white people so well. He saw them close up as a waiter, a shoe shine boy, and as a pimp procuring black women for the kind of white businessmen who complain about welfare rolls and damn permissiveness. His descriptions of the white man are so recognizable that they explain why whites, who would do and be better, still find that they can learn from him.

At a high level of abstraction he wasn't an original thinker. Other black men before him had discussed separatism, nationalism, and power in ways more academically satisfying, but Malcolm actually did these things. His writing about power is uniquely rich and informing when he's on the topic of building a power organization without the white man's money or secret help. He put together a national organization of poor, urban ghetto blacks in the teeth of every sort of hostility.

His device was Islam, first the heterodox variety propounded by the Honorable Elijah Muhammad, and later the one practiced at the Ka'ba. It had a bizarre and dangerous ring to it in the eyes of American whites, but men who have sought to make political and social power with lower-class blacks have frequently found that they had to go out of the nativist traditions. Marcus Garvey drew on the imagery and forms of monarchism almost fifty years ago; the Black Panther party of today leans upon Marxism.

Garvey was destroyed by the government; the

serious potential of an American black Islam ended with Malcolm's murder, and now the Panthers are being squashed with a crude and unlawful whoomp which not even the white and far more dangerously violent Weathermen have been hit with. Yet these are the three most important movements that have been able to recruit, or "fish," as Malcolm said, among the urban masses, so that anyone who wants to work with this group of people almost has to read this book.

This is so whether your intention is political or social-worky. "Every addict takes junk to escape something," writes Malcolm, who took and pushed enough of it to know. ". . . most black junkies are trying to narcotize themselves against being a black man in the white man's America. But, actually . . . the black man taking dope is only helping the white man to 'prove' that the black man is nothing."

If this is true, then these revolutionary new programs for junkie rehabilitation are all a waste of time. More than that. If Malcolm is correct—and there's every reason to believe he is—when the Attorney General smashes black political organizations, he's making customers for the pusher man. Without power to ameliorate the conditions of life, permanent narcosis has its attractions. Yet you might think that to Mr. Mitchell and his gracious, cracker-lady wife who so dreads the coming of the liberal/Communists, this particular Southern strategy would have its drawbacks. The more addicts political hardfistedness creates, the more $50-a-day habits, the more of Mr. Mitchell's rich supporters will be robbed and murdered for their money.

Such are the thoughts that reading Malcolm X's autobiography inspires, but not necessarily. You can find very reassuring and commonplace passages which even the Great Kiwani in the White House can subscribe to: "The polls are one place where every black man could fight the black man's cause with dignity, and with the power and the tools that the white man understands, respects, and fears, and cooperates with . . . In the past, yes, I have made sweeping indictments of *all* white people. I never will be guilty of that again—as I know now that some white people are truly sincere, that some truly are capable of being brotherly toward a black man.''

Malcolm's *hajj,* his pilgrimage to Mecca, taught him that. He was a devout man who chased after God, Allah, and truth with the same unremitting force that he applied to increasing his vocabulary by writing out and committing the dictionary to memory. Islam taught him to be more selective in his denunciations and to yield to the part of his personality that wanted to return good for good. Despite his reputation, he wasn't a hater so much as he was a fighter, and through Islam he learned to distinguish his opponents with more precision.

This change in Malcolm at the end of his life has led to the initiation of a canonization process. People whom he'd have excoriated up and down now have a good word for him. They prefer to forget that on the day of his murder, February 21, 1965, he was the most hated and feared black man in America. If he were alive now, he still would be the most hated and feared, and many who now praise him would not dare.

It was the worst moment for the trial, the worst for the dignity of the court, for the federal judiciary. The chief counsel for the defense was leaning over a desk weeping and imploring the judge to throw him in jail; Jerry Rubin, one of the most lively of the famous seven Chicago conspirators, was standing behind the broken lawyer, clicking his heels together, shouting, "Heil Hitler," and giving Judge Hoffman the Nazi salute; his co-defendant, Dave Dellinger, was calling out, "Leave my daughter alone! They're hurting my daughter!" His daughter, Natasha, and three or four of her friends were fighting off a pack of federal marshals, others were flying onto the pile like red-dogging linebackers, the federal prosecutors were grinning, and the rest of the spectators stood appalled.

The ferocious wee judge had precipitated this latest and most complete destruction of his courtroom. He had begun reading his contempt citations against Dellinger before the jury settled in its place of deliberation, so eager was he to vindicate his dignity against the months that Dellinger had fought him in open court in a manner forbidden to defendants. The judge has a grinding, pedantic voice that makes words by extruding them out from behind locked molars. It frightened people who hoped to escape him and infuriated others who know they are doomed to going to jail whatever they do.

He used the voice to read the citation, particularizing each affront inflicted on his dignity by Dellinger during the nearly five months of the trial. He quoted Dellinger as saying at one point, "You don't want us to have a defense. You're a hypocrite. What Mayor Daley and the police did for the electoral process, you are doing for the judicial process." He rehearsed the number of times Dellinger had refused to rise to his feet when he came into the room, how many times Dellinger had burst out with remarks of protestation, and then he sentenced the man to almost two and a half years in jail.

On the defendants, the net effect was to make them pass through the whole trial experience again, in one compact recapitulation, and they exploded. For other people in the courtroom, it set off the renewed recognition of how different we think our rights are from what we can expect from judges.

Trial by a jury of peers in this case has meant a jury of old people with different backgrounds and beliefs trying young people; it has meant that, before a verdict has been given, the defendants have already been sentenced to a total of thirteen years, three months, and one day in jail for contempt of court. The right to defend oneself has been interpreted to mean sitting gagged and chained to a chair. The right to call witnesses in one's behalf has not been extended to the former Attorney General of the United States, Ramsey Clark, who was sitting and waiting to testify.

All this is legal. All such decisions are discretionary with the judge, the little man who seeks stature through the strength of his marshals. It is they whom he uses to enforce his dignity against the laughter while he sits on his bench explaining how he isn't a racist, but a just, kind, and joking fellow.

He tries to justify himself to a wider audience than his court, but he feels abused in the greater world also. "I have literally thousands of editorials back there in my chamber. I just don't have the time to write letters saying, 'You lied about me' . . . that's the sort of thing that men in public life have to put up with."

The little things are as arbitrary as the big ones.

The young people sleeping on the sidewalks in the freezing weather outside the building wait to get seats in the courtroom, but they are excluded while the judge lets his friends in. When the defense calls him on it, he replies with petulant, over-enunciated diction that "I don't have anything to do with the spectators outside. I have great confidence in the Marshal for the Northern District of Illinois, appointed by the President of the United States. It's his responsibility. We have a system of justice here that takes care of everything."

The courtroom is operated as a system to exact the forms of dignity by a judge who does not return respect with justice. The trial is full of little exchanges like the following.

Mr. Weinglass (defense lawyer): It was my face that Your Honor was reading. I want the record to indicate I was not smiling or laughing.

Judge: The record may show that you are puzzled.

The judge demands not only respect, but love and understanding. "Those who feel ill of me might have a little compassion," he said to Lee Weiner just before sentencing him to jail for contempt. But the defendant replied by telling him that the plaque outside the room at Northwestern University's Law School bearing Julius Hoffman's name had been ripped off the wall by the students there. Did they leave the nameplate on the door? the judge asked.

In such a place, the real issues, legal and political, never get debated. These seven men were indicted for conspiring and the evidence certainly shows they were, but all politics is a conspiracy. What makes this one illegal? Why should it be illegal to do certain things you know your political enemy will overreact to and thereby discredit himself? That is what the defendants did with Mayor Daley. Anyone interested in any kind of political activity in this country needs an answer to that question.

It won't come out of this trial, where the district attorney ends his summation by calling the accused "evil— . . . sophisticated, sociology majors," and promises with a conviction that "the lights in that Camelot will never go out."

The lamp may be burning in Camelot, but sanity is extinguished here. No one knows what to say to this judge. Since the larger questions have disappeared, Tom Hayden, the cerebral radical, tells Hoffman he'd prefer to stay out of jail because "I would like to have a child." One of Abbie Hoffman's last quips is: "The big issue now is prison reform." ▬

Not long ago my eighteen-year-old son told me that he had decided to drop out of college. He'd stuck it out for a year and a half with occasional flashes of enthusiasm but mostly in the spirit of a lovable, faithful, and obedient family dog performing a trick that everybody but he enjoyed. When he informed me of his decision, his voice sounded tired, fagged out.

This happens a lot to parents and children. The children quit; they give up following the career line their parents and the world have prescribed for them. It's usually called rebellion, but if you've talked to many of these kids you'd be more inclined to say it was exhaustion. They remind you less of revoltees than persons who can't go another day, who've tried to hassle it out and only succeeded in progressively dropping to new low levels of spirit and energy.

Calling this dyscrasia of the vital juices rebellion leads parents to apply all the emotional thumb screws—and they have many—to make their large, grown children pick themselves up and go at it again. No middle-class, white American parent can be completely innocent of enjoying the fantasy cocktail party where their son, the Nobel Laureate, is introduced to the neighbors. After all, a guy with a kid who wins a Nobel Prize must have something going for him.

A young man's not so sure he's going to be alive to enjoy the future we're forever urging him to prepare for. Aside from the growing ecological perils which are vivid to young people, there is the draft and the morbid question mark it puts at the end of every thought a young man can have about his hopes and ambitions.

The new law does nothing to eliminate uncertainty. It keeps the old abuses while forcing everybody to play a game of blackjack against the dealer death. Some young people don't mind too much; others can't stand it. For them school becomes a place of compulsion, more of a hide-out against death with the rictus of bureaucracy and lottery on its face than a hideaway for contemplation and learning.

Even without the draft many colleges have become unhappy places. They often are just what their critics say they are, overpeopled, overorganized institutions with too many lines, too much bookkeeping and too many tests. In many places nonpolitical students must tolerate and negotiate the battling and the uproar, the strikes and the sit-ins, the court orders and the expulsions. If you don't have a taste for that kind of life, the sempiternal acrimony on some campuses will drive you out.

There are other elements depressing the blood-sugar count. There is what kids call "irrelevancy." This excessively used and poorly defined word does have a serviceable meaning in relation to education. It can be used to mean that what you learn has no fruitful connection with anything you're likely to do, think or be.

Smarter kids from reasonably good high schools have caught on to the fact that what goes on in many—not all—colleges has an attenuating and vanishing connection with their future work. They see that the B.A. doesn't prepare you to do anything, that it only certifies you as one who no longer has to be kept off the job market and is now employable.

Not too long ago colleges made middle-class ladies and gentlemen. They taught people how to fake it in a white-collar way. This was usually done by putting people through a liberal arts curriculum which was heavily loaded with humanities, the subjects that act as the pumice and polish needed to couth people up.

Increasingly the better high schools have taken over this chore. That's where you now learn the names of the better books and possibly read them. A middle-class youth, especially if he comes from a home where there are lots of books and records and mannered conversation, has already learned the variety of white-collar roles. He knows how teachers, doctors, lawyers, and executives are supposed to behave. He must either begin to learn the substance of these occupations or go out of his mind with this vain, repetitive practice of behavior he's mastered.

College is still a necessary and helpful place for people who've gone to bad schools and come from families where they don't read. It's also a good place for people who want to specialize, particularly if their field of interest demands the use of expensive and elaborate equipment—provided they're allowed to work at their specialty and not be put through years of academic hazing and waiting before they're let at the electron microscope.

For the rest, it's hard to see what they get out

of college. Yet dropping out isn't easy. There's a vast social conspiracy to force a kid onto welfare, into the army, or back to school. A kid with an adequate education—middle-class polish, that is—must learn to lie and affect bad English and lower-class mannerisms if he wants a simple factory job. Personnel managers make a specialty of catching out the "overeducated" and denying them employment. At the same time other personnel managers block them out of the executive trainee program because they haven't served their full four years on the Gothic rock pile.

As long as this state of affairs persists, educational reform of a basic nature is next to impossible. No matter how clever or diverting or entertaining the teachers are, no matter how brain blowing the vis-ed devices and the computer toys, if the schools are stuffed with people who don't want and don't need to be there, you will have trouble but no change on campus. The students will find what they're doing irrelevant because it is, and the only hope we'll have that they don't burn these institutions down is that we can keep them stultified with dope, liquor, sex, athletics, and psychiatric therapy.

The beginning of rational change will come when young people who don't want to go to college are allowed to go to work. That time seems to be receding instead of approaching. There's almost no occupation which isn't busy raising its professional standards, as they like to say, but which really means narrowing the door of entry.

For people like my son this means marginal living. But he's being joined by many, many more. Youthful vagabondage, wandering, catching on here or there for a few days, trying to make it in a commune, three or four people living off the proceeds of one job, moving about, playing music, studying and starving, moping and wondering, trying to start businesses and farms, clogging up whole city neighborhoods, this is becoming more and more common. As a nation we're the old woman who lived in the shoe and even the army has too many young men to know what to do, so we will do nothing about our excess human production.

The best hope is that instead of sitting in on the dean who can't possibly help them, they'll sit in on the employment office and chant, "Give us useful, valuable, dignified work or put us in a real jail." ▬

ith better than 80 per cent of its revenues in war contracts, peace and universal disarmament would be disaster to General Dynamics. Everybody knows that; but peace would be even more devastating to the Peace Movement.

Peace and disarmament would leave General Dynamics with 20 per cent of its business, but it would leave the Movement with nothing. It would be stuck selling a commodity whose value had been destroyed by its abundance. The same observation can be made in almost every line of work.

Cops need crooks; social workers need poverty; teachers need ignorance; trust lawyers need the anti-trust division of the Justice Department; civil rights leaders need Spiro Agnew and the Klan; newspaper writers need the prospect of calamity; cancer researchers need cancer. Almost everybody who's working on a problem has some incentive for failing to solve it.

The unspoken undertow dragging us backward toward failure works with different force on different people. By all rights it should have a

weak pull on the cancer researcher; if he finds a
cure or a preventive, he can pick himself another
disease and go to work again. The radical anti-
war worker, if he's a professional giving his life
to the realization of social change, will be much
slower to welcome the end of hostilities. He
knows the war is making social critics of us all;
it's opening up issue after issue, sensitizing millions of people to exploitations and injustices
they had been oblivious to. He may have de-
cidedly mixed feelings on the day of the cease-
fire, if there is one.

There's a strain of wackiness in these obser-
vations. They violate our notions of social causality. We've been brought up to believe that
history, economics, and society operate in ac-
cordance with set laws like the movements of
heavenly bodies, and the idea of an incentive to
fail doesn't fit in.

It suggests a trace of individual perverseness
that the paradigms by which we explain our collective behavior won't account for. We are most
of us terrible predestinationists who believe human society is out of human control; communist
or capitalist, we don't believe any man can devi-
ate from the path the laws of the market chalk
out for him. Our pessimistic social analyses
predicate impotence and the absence of effective
free will in the creatures who manufacture con-
veyances to the moon.

The exception we allow is something we call
human nature, which is always a bad, bestial
remnant working to reinforce the lugubrious
doom our social systems are preparing for us.
We say it's inherent in the workings of the communist system that the Russians aspire to destroy our freedom; they say it's inherent in the
imperialist system that the Americans want to
steal their money. Then we add that human nature craves the war our societies make inevitable. We sit around and agree that deep inside

our nervous systems, in our gametes and zygotes, down in our very DNA, a territorial imperative drives us to destroy each other.

Man is a naked-ape windup toy.

A lot of this is camouflage to prevent our acknowledging our desire to fail. We wouldn't go to so much trouble only to save our jobs. We want to fail for other and deeper reasons. We are frightened of what success in our major endeavors would bring.

On Sundays we may regard the abolition of war as the commencement of the reign of the Prince of Peace, but the rest of the week permanent, unbroken, universal peace strikes us as a crime against nature, an unnatural act. The oscillating tension between war and peace is like the succession of the seasons to us.

A world at peace is a universal Switzerland; it's Sweden everywhere. There is a permafrost of conviction under the conscious surface that equates peace with declining birthrates, loss of hair and virility, fertility and voluptuousness in women, the end of wit and variety. Peace is perpetually perfect Southern California weather, and we can't stand the thought of it. With final peace would be the end of competition, of drama, of winners and losers. Peace would rob us of our energies and our anxieties.

For us peace would be the peace of the priest who prays, "Requiescat in pace." Peace is death, so we struggle not only for nuclear balance but a balance of peace and war, because we silly things believe war is necessary to keep us alive.

The threat of the abolition of poverty hits us in the same way. "The poor you shall always have with you," we quote to each other, hoping it ever and anon will be so. If peace will rob us of sex and creativity, the demise of poverty will ruin our society.

With the end of poverty the whole system of organized charity will collapse. People use charity, that is, they give other people money as an atonement for their sins, as a way of asserting their superiority over the recipients and as a method of social control. All of this would vanish or be greatly impaired and it scares us.

We can't imagine running a society without a complicated system of deprivations and scarcities to control people. Even now the rich are moaning about the servant problem, how few there are and how poorly they do their jobs. Without poverty who will do the crud work? We don't like to talk about it—it's too unfashionable —but the prospect bothers us so much that we'd rather waste our millions on programs that are designed to fail than face the possibility of success.

These fears don't grow out of a realistic assessment of our economic system but out of our heads. Our fear of peace and prosperity is more theological than pragmatic, so imbued are we with the belief that the natural social life of man is a cycle of constraint, coercion, and punishment. We derive this overview of the necessary human condition from the remains of our fathers' religious beliefs and the rules and truths which were once applicable and reasonable. They aren't any more.

Our social theology is difficult to argue with because it's seldom openly stated. When it is publicly espoused, it's by people like Billy Graham and Norman Vincent Peale who do it in such a noodle-headed way we're ashamed to admit that any part of us responds to the message. Yet these ghosts from the age of scarcity, from the pre-technological epochs interpose themselves between us and reality. They scare us into continuing to see and listen, to think and formulate questions and answers in ways that grow more disastrously risky by the hour.

We must force ourselves to concede that basically new social arrangements do not blaspheme the patriarchal gods. Solving our problems is not spiritual suicide. The end of war won't turn our brains into tepid soup. When our ancestors manumitted the slaves, they thought they were solving what we now are pleased to call the race problem. They didn't. They created a new set of problems which few of them foresaw.

The same will happen with us. We will make new problems for ourselves and that is what we need—new problems. The old dilemmas have been sucked clean of profit. We must erect new walls to butt our heads against. ▰

Many people will keep holiday on Dr. Martin Luther King, Jr.'s birthday. They will not be of one race only. Dr. King had a huge white following when he was alive and has a larger one now, almost two years after his murder. If there are any future historians they may write that he was the most important public figure of his time so that men like John Kennedy, J. Edgar Hoover, Earl Warren, and Bull Connor may be principally remembered for their connection with Dr. King.

He wasn't a man of original thought, not really creative, but he could recognize other people's new ideas and he wasn't too proud to pick them up and use them. He did this with the Student Non-Violent Coordinating Committee. Taking up the ideas which it couldn't disseminate, he propagated them, incorporated them into his own work. SNICK saw the issues first and more clearly, but Dr. King could explain them to millions of people and persuade them to act.

He began as a black leader of black men and

women; on the day of his death he was a black leader of people of all races, and on the question of the Vietnam War his following was principally white. It's only now that blacks in large numbers are starting to manifest opposition to the war.

Some people who admired him said that in a way it was a blessing he died when he did; they said he was slipping, that he was losing his hold on the masses, and that he was too much a rural preacher to be effective in the Northern cities where the worst of the struggle had moved.

Dr. King had these dips in fortune before. His was a leadership that went in alternately bright and dim phases as events and the public mood fluctuated. This is to be expected of a man who wasn't ever able to organize a steady base and whose underlying message always had to overcome his considerable defects as a calculating player of political games.

For all that, he was irreplaceable. When he died his funeral pyre was the burning of twenty American cities.

When men such as Dr. King pass on, their work is uncompleted because what they desire to accomplish is so grandly large. They leave us not so much with work unfinished as with ideals clarified and strengthened. The greatest of these, perhaps, was nonviolence. Dr. King made nonviolence as manly, as courageous an ideal as gun-slinging, although an ideal it remains, given the continued tempo of our murders.

The political murders are the worst. They destroy fidelity and trust like no other crimes. They're never forgotten, and years after the victims have been buried people ruminate over them, feed their paranoia and grudges. Nothing anybody can do can allay such a reaction, but it helps a little if the crimes are as fully and completely explained as is humanly possible.

This is all the more important when there appears to be some substance to the ruminations. Our political murders, at least those of the last decade, all have blacks, liberals, or radicals as their victims. Let's hope it's simply coincidence that Republicans, conservatives, and reactionaries don't get killed, but still the situation is such that the very least that can be done is to put everything that is known about these crimes on the public record.

That hasn't happened with Dr. King. The suspicion persists that James Earl Ray was part of a conspiracy. People like Jack Anderson of the Washington Merry-Go-Round have tried to discourage the talk, saying it's circulated by Dr. King's collaborators in the Southern Christian Leadership Conference to help them raise money, but such scoffing won't sell. The official explanation of how Dr. King was murdered can only be accepted by the gullible and those blessed with great faith in what politicians tell them.

From time to time officials connected with the case have said that Ray did it because he was a racist, but they haven't produced evidence to show he was more of a racist than a lot of other people who don't commit murder. What the record shows is a man who committed crimes for money—a burglar, a robber, and a forger, not an ideologue.

The prosecution contended that this man broke out of the Missouri State Penitentiary in 1967, roamed about the country for a year making his living by crime, and then made his way to Memphis where he stalked Dr. King and killed him. After the murder they say that he escaped to Atlanta, Montreal, London, Lisbon, and then back to London, and he did it all on money he'd either saved up from the profits of older crimes or by committing new ones the particulars of which they're rather vague on.

It may all be true. It's possible, but it gives

James Earl Ray a career profile different from that which most small-time crooks have. Usually this type doesn't make much from their crimes and what they make they spend.

Ray himself has persistently said there was a conspiracy. He said it when he pleaded guilty for the murder and he's said it since. Just because he says it doesn't make it so, but even if he did do it alone there are many questions about how he did it and how he escaped. It was not a simple case, and before he pleaded guilty the prosecution had lined up ninety witnesses to testify to all its puzzling details.

Even the judge, the late W. Preston Battle, confessed there was much which needed explaining: "Like others I would truly like to know how Ray actually found the spot from which to fire. How did Ray know where Rev. King would be? How did he determine the type of weapon to be used? What are the details of the actual purchase and selection of the weapon? Was he alone in surveillance of the Lorraine Motel [where the murder took place]? Most puzzling of all is his escape from Memphis."

The judge wasn't sure that a trial would answer all these questions: "It is an error to assume that the prosecution would have had a chance to cross-examine Ray about his finances or how he escaped from the Missouri State Penitentiary, or about persons who gave him any aid before or after the slaying of Dr. King. That assumes Ray would have taken the stand. I doubt very seriously that defense counsel would have risked placing Ray in such a position. In fact, as I understand it, this all along has been one of the main problems between Ray and various men who have acted for the defense. They counseled against it, and he kept wanting to take the risk."

The lawyers may have been right then, but the trial's over and Ray still wants to talk. He can't be tried again, and he keeps saying from his maximum-security cell that he has a story to tell. It may be that he's some kind of nut. Many people believe he just wants attention and fame. He's already got that. When his bullet struck Dr. King, at that second he got into the history books just as George Wallace did by trying to bar the highway from Selma to Montgomery.

Let a congressional committee subpoena Ray, or give him an opportunity to testify in a court by trying him for a lesser charge like violating Dr. King's civil rights, or form another one of those commissions to take his story down while he stays in the penitentiary, but some way should be found before he's murdered. An administration like the one in office with such a fine nose for conspiracies should be up to the task of determining if there was one here. ■■■

The only air-conditioned forest in New York or maybe in the world flourishes lush in seasonless tranquility inside the Ford Foundation building. Here, azaleas and camellia bushes, jacaranda and magnolia trees grow under a glass-enclosed, man-mastered environment which ends eleven stories above the ground.

In the air-conditioned forest there is a hill and there are pleasant brick pathways which the public may use, although the guards make sure nobody hangs around to eat picnic lunches or play guitars. There is also a pool where people throw coins. These coals-to-Newcastle are fished out because they oxidize and destroy the floating vegetation. After they're retrieved, they're given to local, inconsequential charities, the grubby, Boy Scout sort of thing that the Foundation doesn't bother itself about.

The general effect is like Shangri-la; a place where the corrosive action of nature, where the unfairness of life, where the motion of time with its cycles of death and regeneration are stayed, if not completely abrogated. It is here in quiet glass chambers that the Foundation's four-hundred-plus employees do their serene work of charity, glancing down at the perpetually green forest where it never rains.

This verdant reversal of nature's exigencies is achieved by spending money, lots of it. The Foundation's building, not counting land or furnishings, cost 17 million pre-inflation dollars when it opened in 1967. Since most of the high structure encloses nothing more substantial than artificial sky for the air-conditioned forest, the cost per usable square foot of office space is about $65. This humbling and impressive figure works out to more than $30,000 to house each worker.

The furnishings meet the same high standards of luxury: white oak parquet floors; honey-brown Puerto Rican woven rugs counter-sunk in the floors; silver thermal flasks ($60 per) for the coffee breaks; washable Belgian linen wall coverings; marble steam counter in the cafeteria where the water is drunk from stemware and the food is eaten with simple and handsome silver plate; the Honduran mahogany desks all have steerhide tops, the plainest and smallest of which cost $700 apiece; the elevator interiors also have steerhide walls; the chairs in the board of directors room cost $500 each, while the cafeteria and restaurant, maintained at a huge deficit, are catered by Restaurant Associates, the same people who run the Forum of the Twelve Caesars and The Four Seasons. Lest a visitor draw an erroneous conclusion about that, one of the resident philanthropoids says, "We used to have Voisin handle the food but they weren't satisfactory. That's why we got Restaurant Associates, and you ought to remember, they also own Zum-Zum, the sausage chain."

Nothing has been overlooked. Specially designed typewriter tables, in-and-out bins, desk pen sets, bookends, ashtrays, lamps, and planters—such items are made of marble or architectural bronze, a metal with a deep brass sheen. Indeed, these little details are so attractive that the Foundation has had a pilferage problem, but the management simply orders more rather than permit the employees to violate the decorative scheme with an inharmonious paper-clip tray or unauthorized bud vase. Even the telephones are made to conform—hiding in custom-designed architectural bronze pods flush with the desk tops. The phone system is said to be one of the most complex in the world. It requires a computer to run it, and it is so obedient that you can order it to automatically switch your calls to your home or a hotel.

If the furnishings aren't enough by way of decoration, there are also works of art adorning many of the office walls. They're supposed to be nice but not too splashy, lithographs by Picasso, Miro, and Chagall; lesser-known seventeenth-century Dutch signatures, that kind of thing. It helps to brighten up the building, which costs $700,000 a year to maintain, not counting taxes which the Foundation is exempt from paying.

It's odd that people in Congress and other patriots should be accusing those who work in this palace of stirring up trouble. You'd think that if there ever was a bunch who'd want to keep things just as they are, it would be the campers roughing it in the air-conditioned forest. Instead, Ford's gilded gang is under suspicion of sneaking money to the blacks to liberate themselves. Specifically it's charged that Ford put money into Cleveland in a nonpartisan registration drive which got a lot of black people on the voting rolls and that these people turned around and elected Carl Stokes, the city's first black mayor. If this is true, it would mean that the Foundation violated the one man–no vote formula, and the reactionaries will want to make sure that the staff does nothing more than eat at Le Pavillon.

It's also charged that the Foundation gave money to help the blacks in New York City's Ocean Hill–Brownsville struggle, where the natives attempted to free themselves from the civil service pedagogues who stick like barnacles to the school desks and foreclose the chance the children have of learning something. For this, too, there are Congressmen who want to pass a law prohibiting the Foundation from giving money to government programs which Congress ought to pay for but won't.

For most of the Foundation's existence it has been accused of timidity, excessive caution, and being so coddled in expense accounts, high salaries, and regal living that it was out of contact with the needs of the time. Traditionally it has been taxed for giving alms to academics or high prestige/low popularity cultural endeavors like philharmonic orchestras. They gave away so much money for the playing of archaic music that during the riots one of their own staff members was heard to say, "Ford fiddled while America burned."

It's said that the Foundation broke out of luxury into reality with the advent of its current president, McGeorge Bundy, an ex-presidential assistant who made something of a reputation for himself advising LBJ to get in the war and win it. It's he who led the Foundation into attempting to do some useful things in the area of race relations. In so doing he was implementing the desires of that portion of the American ruling class that is usually called the Eastern Establishment. These are the couth, polished fellows who believe in fair play and enough social change to prevent the mobs on the streets from stealing their money. (The Foundation's all-white board is composed of people like Robert McNamara, Roy E. Larsen, chairman of Time, Inc., plus the heads of a number of other big, profitable organizations.)

They're men who've never stood alone, men who've fled controversy or pioneering, conventional men, the best kind of leaders corporate liberalism has been able to produce. As a collectivity they and their Foundation are tragically late in coming to the realization that we can't return to the 1950's, but they have come to it, and in their well-bred, Ivy League way they've let some money out where it could do a little good.

Now they're being yelled at for it. They won't fight back. They'll collapse. Fighting is in bad taste and when you live in a house like Ford's you put good taste ahead of everything except money. So a good word must be said for them, or the tough guys who knocked them out of control of the Republican party will immobilize them and there will be no hope of them doing what a foundation is supposed to do: be brave, try new things, take a chance. Then McGeorge Bundy will have nothing to do but make modest donations to the Camp Fire Girls who, on national days of participation, might be allowed to have weenie roasts in the ever-green forest. ■■■■

The Black Panther party suggests tough, unusual people. Good tough or bad tough, but tough and smart. That's the way it looks from television when they have those interviews of their leaders, remarkable, self-taught men of the ghetto. Even their enemies build them up. You have to be very high potency to be denounced by J. Edgar Hoover and Evans/Novak.

None of that tells us much about the rank and file. What might the life of a follower be in one of these new Marxist, revolutionary groups? The men and women can't all be like Eldridge and Kathy Cleaver, although for lack of better, closer, and more intimate information we're forced to think they are. This increases our fear and/or respect for the Panthers and allied groups, but not our understanding. It inclines us, if we favor them, to expect more than they can deliver, and, if we're against them, to exaggerate their power.

For this reason Helena's story is useful. Helena is a white college girl who left school to live in a Panther apartment in Harlem while she worked for their allies, the Patriot party, a minuscule hillbilly organization that began in the white slums of Chicago's Uptown district. She's not representative, but even the poor blacks who join a revolutionary party aren't representative. The notion of typicality is a contradiction when thinking about persons engaged in such atypical activities.

Helena's story doesn't tell us everything; it is a fragmented, highly personal, quick look at the ordinary life of the blacks and whites who get caught up in these groups which create a coast-to-coast furor. Helena's name has been changed as have the others who figure in the story, not to protect them politically—certainly the FBI knows them—but to preserve their privacy. Small identifying details have also been altered.

Helena is twenty-three, a small-town girl whose father is a local merchant, a country-club member, a Chamber of Commerce, Kiwanis club man, a VFW regular. She's an only child, and a pretty girl whose parents continue to send her $40 a week believing she's still attending school.

In some ways she reminds you of many young women in her fear that there is no work for her to do.

"I'm an extremely passionate human being, and when I do something that's dangerous and risky, that's when I feel alive. I wanted to discover what other kinds of people are like," Helena says. And so she followed the Panthers and the Patriots to New York after some of them had come to her campus to stir up support.

When Helena and her friend Daphne got to New York the actual situation was different from the tight organization they had envisioned. The Patriot party was almost nonexistent. Its leader wasn't a poor white, much less a hillbilly, but a young lawyer named Burt. "He wore the whole uniform," says Helena, "the combat boots, black leather jacket, and buttons. Burt would always talk about how a real man knows how to handle a piece [gun], but when we finally did recruit a heavy, white street cat, who'd served five years for murder, Burt was afraid of him."

The Patriot organization that the two girls found in New York was dependent on the Panthers. It had no headquarters and no apartment until it moved in on a taxicab driver. "Really, it was mostly women. There were only two layable men, Burt and the street cat who came later. The other two males were fifteen and seventeen and not attractive. The cab driver was a real sickie. He'd walk around naked and leave the bathroom door open so you had to see him."

Much of Burt's time, according to Helena, was taken up with the Patriots' headquarters in Chicago, where it appeared Burt was not much appreciated because "they were into 'Possum Nationalism,'" meaning they didn't want any non-hillbillies in their organization. Furthermore, they seemed to be relapsing out of Marxism, having second thoughts about being a national political party, and wanting to return to being a street-corner, neighborhood bottle gang. For his part, Burt didn't think too much of them because they had a democratically elected central committee which is anathema to Burt's kind of Stalinistic Maoism. "Burt would say that people who elect their leaders won't take orders from them."

The first month was enjoyable, even though Burt appropriated Helena's car "for the people," which meant she and the others walked while Burt drove around the city.

She and Daphne lived in a Panther apartment because "There was no Patriot place for us to stay, so Daphne and I said, 'This is supposed to be a rainbow coalition, we'll live in a Panther crib.' "

It wasn't an easy situation. As Helena says, "If you want privacy, you're not a Communist." She says her friend Daphne didn't want privacy and resolved the difficulties of being an attractive, unattached woman by "passing her bod around." Helena, however, met Freddie, a nineteen-year-old but still veteran Panther, and the two fell in love.

The days were busy past exhaustion. First there was political education, called PE by the membership. "We had to know [Mao Tse-tung's] Red book and its definitions of the five points of attention and the eight points of something else," says Helena. "They use the political dialectic thing on everything, even to resolving personal conflict. They call it 'waging struggle,' like a person would say, 'We're waging struggle about whose peanut-butter sandwich this is.' "

There was no money. Helena couldn't use her allowance because she didn't want her parents to see the checks had been cashed in New York. "Sometimes we had to panhandle to buy paper for the leaflets we mimeographed at St. Mark's Church. That's a really hip church where two white wives of Panther members run the party's free breakfast program for the kids. I'd walk up to somebody and say, 'Can I have a dollar, please? I'm hungry.' The Patriots had a little treasury which was supposed to be for party work. I didn't know that some of them were taking money for cigarettes, food, carfare, and Tampax.

"It's very hard to be a revolutionary when you can't live off the land. Money dragged us down. Not eating, no medicine. I fainted one time at Columbia selling newspapers in the rain."

Having no paper of their own, the Patriots sold the Panther paper for a quarter apiece. Without carfare and with Burt using "the people's car," Helena had to walk back and forth across Manhattan selling her quota of seventy or eighty papers a day. "We made a big hit as the first white women to sell the Black Panther paper," she remembers. "I'd have to scrape the spit off my coat. The way we'd do it is we'd just get out there and scream. 'Do you know what they did to my chairman? If they do it again we'll blow their heads off!' When I'd do it, sometimes I'd joke with the pigs. There was one very nice pig, but we weren't supposed to treat a pig like a human being."

It was a life of ill health and marginal hunger. "I caught something that sounds like trichinosis —trichi-something because I wasn't eating or bathing. You just get used to being funky. I hated it, actually. Those dirty sheets, the bugs. If I'd been younger I'd have found it exciting, but I was too old for it. Once I had something venereally wrong with me. I felt awful and I went to the apartment of this liberal doctor who helped the party. It was sumptuous, and there in this apartment some Panthers were having this absolutely gorgeous dinner. I thought, 'I hate these people!' I was so hungry, so dirty. I got mad because there were ex-Panthers there too and you're not supposed to talk to ex–party members."

The situation in the Panther apartment was

very upsy-downsy. "The house captain was a maniac. He wasn't a racist, though. He treated everybody like he treated me. Freddie and I almost never had any time alone. He'd come in and putter around when Freddie and I might not have seen each other for two days. We were living on three hours sleep. We were always exhausted, but the house captain would come into the room in the middle of the night screaming, 'The spirit of the people will keep you warm. Clean the bathroom!' Then four or five Panther chicks would come in and say, 'This is a Panther crib. We'll crash here.'

"It got to the point I just couldn't get up in the morning. The captain would stand up over my bed and scream. I was afraid to go to sleep. And we always stayed up late even when there wasn't anything to do because there was always a fight —sorry, I mean a struggle—and if it wasn't that, it was the possibility of a raid by the pigs so we'd have to stay up with our pieces, two guns, one of which didn't work."

In the end, Helena says, both the Panthers and the Patriots moved to break up her romance on the grounds that, variously, "Helena was pulling down Freddie's PE level, that the Harlem community wasn't ready to accept an interracial couple, that they were relating to each other individually instead of politically." Helena doesn't believe it but blames the Panther chicks and the Patriot men.

They quit their respective parties and Freddie came back to the college town to live with Helena, but it didn't work out. He was outside his milieu, and after years of having a mission and a place in the order of things, he was without anything to do. As Helena says, "Quitting the party is like coming off heroin."   ▄▄

In the second installment of his new Mission Impossible television series, actor-statesman LBJ was heard and seen to cry out against those who deserted him when he went to war. It would have been different, and so much better, he wailed, if the country had only rallied behind him, if we'd grown vegetables in victory gardens and Boy Scouts had gone door to door peddling savings bonds.

That was not to be, because either he or his highest subordinates had lied, misrepresented, and contradicted themselves so often and so seriously that only the unthinkingly obedient could believe Vietnam to be a high patriotic endeavor. This would not be so important save that the war goes on and our men must give their lives and we our money for "Vietnamization" where once we were asked to do so because radar blips suggested our destroyers might have been attacked in the Tonkin gulf, where later it was because the Secretary of State was playing dominoes, and later yet it was treaty commitments and after that it was to repel aggression and then it was for free elections and so on.

It is one thing to be young and to give your life for your country and another to die for such an ugly and undefinable word as "Vietnamization." It has too many letters in it to be accommodated on the modest headstones of our soldiers' graves.

The incongruity of dying for such a twerpish semantic notion as Vietnamization underscores the difficulty of pursuing a foreign policy, even a wise one, that has no support at home. From 1940 until LBJ fell on his face in the Big Muddy, an American President could do anything abroad and count on a pliant, if not always enthusiastic, nation to back him up. That's over, as this administration too will find out now that it has made it clear that it is willing to go on fighting for years and years.

One of the places where the disgust and languor causes the most trouble is the armed forces. The Army shouldn't be blamed for the war, but they are. They know it and they, poor things, are trying to adjust their sales pitch. The new radio advertisements for the National Guard imply if you join up you'll never see a rifle but will spend most of your time rescuing people from floods, feeding cattle marooned in snow storms, comforting orphans, and fighting juvenile delinquency. The Air Force ads invite you to sign up for a life of scientific research work, while the Army seems to be saying, "We're not asking you to enlist to fight, but to matriculate to learn, and get a pension at the same time."

The unpopularity of what the armed forces are being asked to do is so great that Washington chitchat has it that many upper-level officers find it uncomfortable to wear their uniforms on the street and to social occasions where they risk meeting strangers with hostile opinions. Lower down, men doubt themselves and the rightness of what they're doing.

Not all the doubters are tilted toward the left. *Triumph,* a very conservative Roman Catholic monthly, has a long and sympathetic story in this month's issue about an Air Force officer resigning his post as a Minuteman II crew commander. As a serious working Roman Catholic, Major Robert C. Margetts decided he could not conscientiously execute the government's Emergency War Order, the instructions under which the Air Force is supposed to kill the civilian population of Russia in the event of war. Citing his church's teaching that such acts are "a crime against God and man himself," the major offered to fight in Vietnam.

"I could have kept my moral reservations to

myself and spent two more years on a missile
crew and could have depended on a normal career progression and a nice retirement. But then
I felt it was my duty, my honor, to reveal this to
my superiors," he wrote—but the top brass
seemed to think he was no longer reliable, and,
instead of taking him up on his offer to go off to
war, honorably discharged him.

At the other end of the continuum of doubt,
scruples, and disinterest in our military doings
are the twenty-seven men at the Presidio military
stockade who were court-martialed for mutiny.
Fred Gardner has written a first-rate study of this
case, The Unlawful Concert (Viking Press, New
York, $5.95). He is one of the founders of the GI
coffee-house movement, a person who for four
years has worked with and gotten to know many
enlisted men, the draftee soldiers who must go,
like it or not.

He sums up the mutineers by saying they were
"all white. Their average age was nineteen, their
median educational level tenth grade. Fourteen
of them came from disrupted families. Almost all
had enlisted to get out of trouble or to learn a
trade, five under duress, seven having been misled by a recruiter's pitch. They were AWOL's,
and almost all from small towns. None had been
political in civilian life, though four had been
vaguely anti-war before coming into the service.
Eight more became deeply anti-war during their
stints."

These young men weren't in the stockade accused of committing any criminal acts, just for
being AWOL, and that in itself is a tipoff. Gardner writes, "There were 53,357 desertion cases
in the Armed Services in fiscal 1968 and 155,536
AWOLS—the equivalent of fifteen combat divi-
sions and more than five times the number of
men volunteering for Vietnam duty. In the Army
alone, someone was leaving every three minutes."

In addition to these men there are an estimated ten thousand others in Canada and elsewhere escaping the draft, and unknown, probably very large numbers, who, true to their middle-class training, trot along into the Army, but, true to their own lack of conviction, pull their time doing as little as possible.

Another indication is the tone of the complaints about conditions within the army. Here we have former private Andy Stapp writing (*Up Against the Brass,* Simon and Schuster, New York). Stapp, a radical who accepted induction so he could organize the American Servicemen's Union, writes as follows of Fort Sill, Oklahoma, and its symbiotic garrison town of Lawton:

"I was assigned to the Army's ration breakdown section. From 7 A.M. to 5 P.M. we delivered rations to the mess halls in two-and-a-half-ton trucks. What we were actually doing, however, was helping the mess sergeants and the mess officer . . . We were told to falsify records for them. If a particular mess hall fed one hundred men, we were told to claim it fed one hundred and fifty."

Other complaints aren't new—the venality of the little garrison towns with their rows of tarts and dirty bookstores, the stupidity among lifer NCO's, the low pay of the enlisted men and the very real hardships it frequently causes their families. (Some of the saddest AWOL cases concern men who've gone over the hill to get jobs to support their wives and children.)

None of these things are new. What's new is the general indisposition to overlook them, to discount them as the price we have to be willing to pay to win a war, to blind ourselves to them because our eyes and our attentions are fixed on a higher cause. But Vietnamization isn't a cause. It's a chronic affliction, one that makes men look around to see what's wrong and fashion grudges, or try to figure out how to beat the system.

And not all regard the man who does beat the system as shameful, or call him a slacker or a coward or a malingerer. He may be looked on as a lucky one. The January 31, 1970, issue of the *New Republic* has an article called "The Man Who Beat the Army," which tells how a soldier squeaked out of being sent to the front almost at gunpoint. It also points out he was older and had more than average savvy and $6,000 to spend on lawyers' fees. It quotes him as saying, "If I'd been a green kid, broke, just out of high school and basic training, I'd still be in jail."

Thousands are. Kidding them that the armed forces are humanitarian enterprises or are really schools where the students are disguised as soldiers isn't going to shake their lassitude. Nor are we going to get much more from an army that gets its men by giving them a choice of enlisting or involuntary commitment to an insane asylum, as happened in one case that Gardner cites.

Neither pep talks nor presidential press conferences plugging Vietnamization will change any of this. America's fanny is dragging.

I

It is impossible to date a mood, a psychological era. But if the beginnings are lost it is retrospectively obvious that some time in the middle years of this decade we began to feel differently about ourselves. We began to relish and cultivate a sense of doom and revenge; we spoke of the Fire Next Time and we liked the feelings the thought of fear induced in us; we spoke of Armageddon and Apocalypse like people who wanted what the rest of mankind dreads.

We ascended the helix of violence, crime, confrontation, counter-confrontation, riot, arson, and assassination as though we were going through a sexual experience. We enjoyed it. We proclaimed ourselves the sick society with a necrophiliac delight in the pathology of pathology. After each act of bloodletting we were not content with seeing it on the TV screen; we had commissions to dredge it up again, show us the killing in new lights, and use the analysis of the largest acts of savagery as grounds to predict yet more. Our violence commissions and their reports never lead to legislation—their function is to soothsay the doom we delight in hearing prognosticated.

In the last months new elements have become discernible in the mood. The first is suspicion. There are now millions of people who believe their phones are being tapped. Congressmen, senators, high government and business officials presume it in their belief that the government is increasingly in the hands of spies and blackmailers. In the most unlikely and exalted places there is talk of repression and concentration camps.

The second is the talk of revolution. Six or seven years ago only paranoid reactionaries gabbled about revolution. For everybody else the subject was laughable. Now the word is used everywhere and all the time, and not merely as metaphor or hyperbole as in the Dodge Rebellion or the Sexual Revolution.

People say the word again and again, meaning they expect in some vague, indefinite, but not too far future time a violent political upheaval will come to pass. The word is tossed around thoughtlessly but with the connotation that it will solve our problems, take care of everything, make us well. If you try to pin people down as to how this last and most awful political act is going to make anything better, you don't get answers; you get emotional expectations. Their words in reply suggest that a great welling up and solidifying of masses of people will provide a purging, a burning, and a purification of the great, collective, social soul. They talk like people drained of energy who see the revolution as a dynamo of massive, undifferentiated human force which recharges and revives them.

Such talk centers among the rich and the near rich. It began among the young but it's spread to the parents and the grandparents, so you can hear dowager millionairesses drop casual remarks about the revolution.

The prevalency of revolutionary talk has sprung up in two or three years. Maybe it's simply a fashion and, like bell-bottom trousers, people will tire of it, but that's not certain. We don't know much about revolutions, but what we do know makes it impossible to shrug off the conversations as having no consequence.

It has been observed that no government or master class has ever been overthrown from below. They've committed suicide. (We're speaking of true revolutions, not putsches, coups d'état, or CIA palace takeovers.) The rulers, the rich, the people with presumably the most stake in the status quo lose faith in themselves and belief in the goodness and worthwhileness of both their duties and their heritage.

The revolutionary talk isn't coming primarily from blacks or white factory workers or Mexican farm labor but from the top, from people with money and people with means to broadcast their ideas and convince others. It is this fact that makes it highly unlikely that, the Constitution aside, the government will indulge in the wholesale political repressions that are forever being predicted. The government isn't going to put its own children in jail. Black Panthers, of course, are a totally different question.

This rage for revolution, so common in the

Western world, derives from feelings and beliefs that are often admirable and courageous. When you see a Sarah Lawrence girl or a Yale boy working on a production line to start a revolutionary cadre, it's hard not to salute them for their selflessness, but their altruism doesn't make what they're doing less reckless or badly thought-out.

"We know to our sorrow that freedom has been better preserved where no revolution ever broke out, no matter how outrageous the circumstances of the powers that be, and that there exist more civil liberties even in countries where the revolution was defeated than in those where the revolutions have been victorious," writes Hannah Arendt in one of the few good books on the subject (*On Revolution,* Viking Press, New York, 1965, $1.65).

But people with the revolutionary rage in them take freedom and civil liberties for granted in their justifiable anguish over such questions as racism, war, and poverty. What they forget is that there is no reason to think pulling down the formal, governmental structure of the country can solve these problems while there is every reason to believe a revolution will add new ones.

The great problem a revolution would bring with it would be the establishing of any other kind of government that the American people could accept as legitimate. It doesn't matter how much good can be said for it; the fact is that every revolutionary government goes through the tortures of the damned trying to achieve the legitimation and acceptance which bring stability and the possibility of going forward with any kind of social or economic program.

The legitimation of the American government is the Constitution, a document which we revere with considerably greater and realer piety than we do our various religions. We do it not only because it actually is an amazing political creation but because it is nearly two hundred years old, and we believe in it in a sense that is more than patriotic, more than governmental. It cannot be replaced by something better because we believe in it, our Constitution, nobody else's, and it is this which gives the system legitimate authority, stability, and therefore the possibility of quiet and humane improvement and perfection.

One of the most alarming aspects of the kind of talk we're getting now is a discrediting attack on the Constitution's authority. Arendt puts it this way: "Revolutions always appear to succeed with amazing ease in their initial stage, and the reason is that the men who make them first only pick up the power of a regime in plain disintegration; they are consequences but never the causes of the downfall of political authority . . . The loss of authority in the powers-that-be, which indeed precedes all revolutions, is actually a secret to no one, since its manifestations are open and tangible, though not necessarily spectacular; but its symptoms, general dissatisfactions, widespread malaise, and contempt for those in power, are difficult to pin down since their meaning is never unequivocal."

That's where we are now. The Constitution, our stabilizer, our continuity, our guarantee of freedom for those who have it and our promise for those who don't, is suffering authority drainage. But as Miss Arendt says, the picture is equivocal. the revolutionary enragees bring the final and binding laws into contempt, but so does the Attorney General who is reported smiling while his wife runs off at the mouth at parties making tasteless, racist imitations of somebody speaking Swahili.

If you think you're a revolutionary, know what you're getting all of us into, and if you're not, don't talk like one.

As the fashion for revolutionary talk has taken hold of growing portions of our middle- and upper-class population, the hope for social and personal salvation through upheaval has linked itself to the black and the poor. It is as though the rich, especially the young rich, tired in spirit, bereft of hope in their own way of life, seek to be baptized anew in the revolutionary blood and energy of the poor.

Hannah Arendt calls this amalgam of zeal, sympathy, altruism, and exhaustion of the soul "the passion for compassion." She says of this emotion that ". . . it will shun the drawn-out wearisome processes of persuasion, negotiation, and compromise, which are the processes of law and politics and lend its voice to the suffering itself, which must claim for swift and direct action, that is, for action with the means of violence."

This may make psychic sense for well-to-do whites who're so desiccated within they must discover and live off of black soul, but attacking the political structure of a society for whatever internal spiritual needs isn't likely to help poor people. Formal political organization, government in the legal, juridical, and institutional sense of the word, is a sloppy and unpromising instrument for dealing with poverty. Yet the anger of passion for compassion frustrated is targeting itself on government, not on economics, not on the systems and arrangements that perpetuate want and material degradation in this land of elusive abundance.

At the same time there is an excruciating political problem for the poor and the not so poor. It's the problem of purely political powerlessness. It's terribly serious, but the only politician to make so much as an attempt to do anything about it in recent years has been George Wallace, a man who—his racism aside—has good instincts for the widespread feeling of civic deprivation in our country.

He is not the first American politician to note it. Miss Arendt quotes John Adams on the subject as follows, "The poor man's conscience is clear; yet he is ashamed . . . He feels himself out of the sight of others, groping in the dark. Mankind takes no notice of him. He rambles and wanders unheeded. In the midst of a crowd, at church, in the market . . . he is in as much obscurity as he would be in a garret or a cellar. He is not disapproved, censured, or reproached; *he is only not seen* . . . To be wholly overlooked, and to know it, are intolerable."

This is the silent American, some of whom George Wallace has tried to speak for. They are poor whites in the political sense of poor; they have no real equity in the country. Notice when he talks about this constituency of his, he usually mentions that they are small farmers, cab drivers, insurance workers, factory operatives, people perhaps with jobs but no real leverage. Unhappily, for Wallace black people are still unseen and as a consequence what he likes to call his movement is out of phase with our most pressing case of disfranchisement.

Many others of us hear this talk about silent America and we get frightened. We disbelieve. We say that's malarky because people have the vote. For a long time Wallace has understood that the vote alone can be a trick to make people think they have political power when they have none. Again and again he's pointed out how essentially this is a one-party nation, a country ruled by Demopubs or Reprocrats. He's never compared it to Russia, another one-party state, but the temptation is too great to forgo.

Miss Arendt has this to say about the vote: "Jefferson, though the secret vote was still unknown at the time, had at least a foreboding of how dangerous it might be to allow the people a share in public power without providing them at the same time with more public space than the ballot box and with more opportunity to make their voices heard in public than on election day. What he perceived to be the mortal danger to the republic was that the Constitution had given all power to the citizens, without giving them the opportunity of *being* citizens and of *acting* as citizens."

People in the political predicament just described are highly susceptible to being turned into mobs, and rabbles, stomping, lynching silent majorities, ghetto-burning berserkers. This administration and the last have both proven adept at doing just that. The Kennedy-Johnsonians incited blacks and other oppressed people to the highest political sensitivity without attempting to build a method by which they could act as citizens; the Nixonians are doing the same with the factory workers, the Wallace clientele.

The result is confusion, contradiction, George Gallup, Lou Harris, and a growing mood of violence and tension which is in itself not revolutionary but which revolutionary currents can amplify and make dangerous. "In this system," writes Hannah Arendt, "the opinions of the people are indeed unascertainable for the simple reason that they are nonexistent. Opinions are formed in a process of open discussion and public debate, and where no opportunity for the forming of opinions exists, there may be moods —moods of the masses and moods of individuals, the latter no less fickle and unreliable than the former—but no opinion."

There's no reason for this. There's no reason for the wild fluctuations in public opinion polls so they'll register 80 per cent of the people taking diametrically opposite positions on successive months. People are not stupid or flighty, but they haven't had the chance to debate and listen and form settled, knowledgeable opinions. It need not be. We read Jefferson and we understand how remediable this vat of brawling, broiling contention is: "As Cato concluded every speech with the words, *Carthago delenda est,* so do I every opinion with the injunction, 'divide the counties into wards' . . . small republics . . . The elementary republics of the wards, the county republics, the State republics, and the republic of the Union would form a graduation of authorities, standing each on the basis of law, holding every one its delegated share of powers, and constituting truly a system of fundamental balances and checks for the governments."

Over and over people in this country and abroad have combined to make small, neighborhood, self-governing republics or councils or whatever you want to call them, and they've been crushed. Miss Arendt points out how Lenin did it to the Soviets, the Russian neighborhood organizations, and if she had written later she could point out how Congresswoman Edith Green, a person who's described as a liberal Democrat, has led the fight to make sure OEO didn't encourage the development of local organizations here.

Time after time in housing, police administration, schools, the administration of welfare, people in America have tried to build local units of self-government where they can act as citizens, debate, make decisions, and just as often they've been stopped by Democrats or Republicans—Reprocrats all who believe the party knows best. The party doesn't, though, Bolsheviks or Reprocrats, and the result of their fumbling and flaying are schemes of successively worse efficacy and rationality, each costing more and getting less done.

Having gutted the healthy foundations of a sane and sober political life at the neighborhood level, the Reprocrat leaders go about making speeches and conducting hearings on what? Party Reform! And while they execute these delusional maneuvers, the chaos, the crime, and the resentment grows. Southern strategies, Northern strategies, nobody is placated. And everywhere the cry is "build more jails, get more judges, hire more cops," and at the cocktail parties and all the smart places, even the rich complain of their impotency and go yatata-yatata about the coming revolution.   ▄▄▄

Nicholas von Hoffman was born in New York City, worked with Saul Alinsky's Industrial Areas Foundation, and reported for the *Chicago Daily News* before he joined the *Washington Post*, where he is now cultural affairs editor. Mr. von Hoffman is the author of *Two, Three, Many More; We Are the People Our Parents Warned Us Against; The Multiversity;* and *Mississippi Notebook.*